T0399735

Routledge Philosophy Guidebook to

Spinoza on Politics

Baruch Spinoza is one of the most influential and controversial political philosophers of the early modern period. Though best known for his contributions to metaphysics, Spinoza's *Theological-Political Treatise* (1670) and his unfinished *Political Treatise* (1677) were widely debated and helped to shape the political writings of philosophers as diverse as Rousseau, Kant, Marx, Nietzsche, and (although he publicly denied it) even Locke. In addition to its enormous historical importance, Spinoza's political philosophy is also strikingly contemporary in its advocacy of toleration of unpopular religious and political views and his concern with stabilizing religiously diverse democratic societies.

The first guidebook to Spinoza's political writings, *The Routledge Philosophy Guidebook to Spinoza on Politics* covers the following key points:

- Spinoza's life and the background to his philosophy
- the key themes and arguments of the *Theological-Political Treatise* and *Political Treatise*
- the continuing importance of Spinoza's work to philosophy.

This book is an ideal starting point for anyone new to Spinoza and essential reading for students of political philosophy and seventeenth-century philosophy.

Daniel Frank is Professor of Philosophy at Purdue University, USA and has published widely on Greek and medieval Jewish philosophy.

Jason Waller is Assistant Professor of Philosophy at Eastern Illinois University, USA. He is the author of a number of articles on Spinoza, as well as *Persistence through Time in Spinoza* (2012).

ROUTLEDGE PHILOSOPHY GUIDEBOOKS

Edited by Tim Crane and Jonathan Wolff

University of Cambridge and University College London

Plato and the *Trial of Socrates* Thomas C. Brickhouse and Nicholas D. Smith
Aristotle and the *Metaphysics* Vasilis Politis
Rousseau and the *Social Contract* Christopher Bertram
Plato and the *Republic*, second edition Nickolas Pappas
Husserl and the *Cartesian Meditations* A.D. Smith
Kierkegaard and *Fear and Trembling* John Lippitt
Descartes and the *Meditations* Gary Hatfield
Hegel and the *Philosophy of Right* Dudley Knowles
Hegel and the *Phenomenology of Spirit* Robert Stern
Berkeley and the *Principles of Human Knowledge* Robert Fogelin
Aristotle on Ethics Gerard Hughes
Hume on Religion David O'Connor
Leibniz and the *Monadology* Anthony Savile
The Later Heidegger George Pattison
Hegel on History Joseph McCarney
Hume on Morality James Baillie
Hume on Knowledge Harold Noonan
Kant and the *Critique of Pure Reason* Sebastian Gardner
Mill on Liberty Jonathan Riley
Mill on Utilitarianism Roger Crisp
Spinoza and the *Ethics* Genevieve Lloyd
Heidegger on *Being and Time*, second Edition Stephen Mulhall
Locke on Government D.A. Lloyd Thomas
Locke on *Human Understanding* E.J. Lowe
Derrida on Deconstruction Barry Stocker
Kant on Judgement Robert Wicks
Nietzsche on Art Aaron Ridley
Rorty and the *Mirror of Nature* James Tartaglia
Hobbes and *Leviathan* Glen Newey
Wittgenstein and the *Tractatus* Michael Morris

Aristotle and the *Politics* Jean Roberts
Merleau-Ponty and *Phenomenology of Perception* Komarine Romdenh-Romluc
Frege on *Sense and Reference* Mark Textor
Kripke and *Naming and Necessity* Harold Noonan
Kant on *Religion within the Boundaries of Mere Reason* Lawrence Pasternack
Wittgenstein and *On Certainty* Andy Hamilton

Routledge Philosophy Guidebook to

Spinoza on Politics

Daniel Frank and Jason Waller

LONDON AND NEW YORK

First published 2016
by Routledge
2 Park Square, Milton Park, Abingdon, Oxon OX14 4RN

Simultaneously published in the USA and Canada
by Routledge
711 Third Avenue, New York, NY 10017

Routledge is an imprint of the Taylor & Francis Group, an informa business

© 2016 Daniel Frank and Jason Waller

The rights of Daniel Frank and Jason Waller to be identified as the authors
of this work have been asserted by them in accordance with sections
77 and 78 of the Copyright, Designs and Patents Act 1988.

All rights reserved. No part of this book may be reprinted or reproduced or
utilised in any form or by any electronic, mechanical, or other means, now
known or hereafter invented, including photocopying and recording, or
in any information storage or retrieval system, without permission in
writing from the publishers.

Trademark notice: Product or corporate names may be trademarks or
registered trademarks, and are used only for identification and
explanation without intent to infringe.

British Library Cataloguing in Publication Data
A catalogue record for this book is available from the British Library

Library of Congress Cataloging in Publication Data

ISBN: 978-0-415-55606-4 (hbk)
ISBN: 978-0-415-55607-1 (pbk)
ISBN: 978-1-315-69639-3 (ebk)

Typeset in Garamond
by Taylor & Francis Books

for Jan Cover

CONTENTS

	Preface	x
	Abbreviations	xiii
1	The Theological-Political Problem	1
2	Naturalism, Right, and Power	13
3	The State of Nature and the Origins of Civil Society	28
4	Critique of Traditional Biblical Religion	45
5	The Universal Religion	91
6	Toleration	107
7	Democratic Theory	133
	Bibliography	153
	Index	161

Preface

This book is an introduction to Spinoza's political philosophy. In the history of modern political philosophy Spinoza's work tends to be overlooked. In the tradition that commences with Hobbes – or sometimes Machiavelli – the story proceeds quickly, too quickly, to Locke, Hume, Rousseau, Kant, and Hegel. The classical liberalism of Hobbes and Locke grounds political sovereignty in a social contract. Thinkers in this tradition tend to argue for a state that is scrupulously neutral with respect to competing conceptions of the good life. By the time of the French Revolution at the end of the eighteenth century, however, political theory begins to move along robust communitarian and republican lines. The state is taken to play a far more active and positive role in the lives and destinies of its citizens. This popular story of modern political thought from classical liberalism to classical republicanism is incomplete, however, without an appreciation of the crucial contribution that Spinoza makes. Spinoza's view is neither a liberal social contract theory nor a version of classical republicanism. Instead his political philosophy shares features of both traditions, and so is a kind of bridge between them. Disagreeing in important ways with Hobbes while anticipating eighteenth-century Enlightenment trends, we denominate Spinoza's view "Liberal Republicanism".

Liberal Republicanism promotes a positive role for the state in the inculcation of a set of distinctively liberal virtues in the citizenry. Such a position is not neutral with respect to competing conceptions of the good life in the way that classical liberalism requires, but neither does it attempt to inculcate *all* virtues as the classical republican tradition requires. Rather Spinoza's Liberal Republicanism seeks to inculcate only those virtues necessary to allow a pluralistic and democratic state to function. First and foremost amongst these virtues is tolerance, and its promulgation is for Spinoza key to peace and harmony in a pluralistic state.

In our book we spend much time, as one must, on the role of religion in the state. *Prima facie* it is curious that Spinoza, an atheist if ever there was one, finds an important role for religion in the state. But Spinoza is a realist about human nature, and his pessimism entails that religion and the values it stands for be taken on by the political sovereign as a most significant tool in fostering peace in the state. We emphasize the role that civil religion plays in Spinoza's political thought because we are keen to distance ourselves from the common view that takes Spinoza as a thoroughgoing anti-religious thinker, committed to a strict separation of Church and State. To be sure, he wishes to put the Church under the strict control of the sovereign political power, and in so doing to limit the power and influence of the former, but Spinoza's deep pessimism about human nature and the abiding power of superstition and the passions in human life requires that religion and its values find their place within the state.

As noted, Spinoza is a bridge figure in modern political philosophy, but he is also in his own way the final act in the pre-modern political philosophical tradition, commencing with Plato and running right through the medieval period of natural and revealed law and prophetic revelation. We spend rather less time on his role as spoiler of this tradition, but it does find voice in his radical biblical hermeneutics. Spinoza is a fierce critic of traditional religion and its approach to Scripture, and we try to clarify how his biblical hermeneutics serves his own revisionist *political* agenda. For Spinoza, the Bible is a repository of moral wisdom and cautionary political tales, but no more than this. It is manifestly not the foundation for political authority. Spinoza founds the state upon a rather pessimistic

xii PREFACE

view of human nature and the universal striving for self-preservation. But these seemingly Hobbesian starting points are entirely reworked by Spinoza on account of his own views of freedom and bondage. The Spinoza who emerges from these pages is a political philosopher of the first rank, a representative of his troubled time and place in the seventeenth-century Dutch Republic, and one who anticipates by over a century the democratic trends of the eighteenth-century French Enlightenment.

As part of the Routledge Philosophy Guidebook series, this book is intended as an introduction to the subject. While it engages current scholarly debates, it does so selectively and without explicitly signaling such with footnotes. To direct the reader to recent work on specific topics, each chapter concludes with some suggestions for further reading. Recent work by Curley, Rosenthal, Steinberg, Nadler, Rutherford, Garrett, and Israel has been especially useful to us. We have also been helped by seeing Spinoza's theorizing in the context of important work on perfectionism and liberalism by Raz, Sher, Wall, Galston, and Hurka. We find real similarities in their respective critiques of state neutrality with respect to promulgating virtue and a conception of the good and Spinoza's own view of the role that the liberal state ought to play in the lives of its citizens.

We thank Tony Bruce and Adam Johnson at Routledge for their encouragement and patience, and for forwarding the very helpful comments of two anonymous reviewers, which aided us in the course of revision. In addition, each of us has a few people to thank for discussion and support during the writing of this book. Daniel Frank thanks Chris Yeomans, and especially Joshua Frank and Lynn Parrish for responding to innumerable queries and simply for being there when necessary. Jason Waller thanks Mickey Lorkowski, Hans Lottenbach, Grant Sterling, Yang Xiao, Tim Shutt, Lisa Leibowitz, Bailey Young, and especially Rebecca Lloyd Waller, whose philosophical acumen and kindness continue to be a source of inspiration. We also acknowledge the contributions of the students we have taught at Purdue, Eastern Illinois, Kentucky, and Kenyon.

We dedicate our book to an extraordinary colleague and teacher, whose scholarship is impeccable and whose friendship endures.

ABBREVIATIONS

The following abbreviations are used in citations of Spinoza's texts:

E   *Ethics* (trans. E. Curley, 1985)
         c   corollary
         d   definition (not following a proposition number)
                   demonstration (following a proposition number)
         exp.   explanation
         p   proposition
         pref.   preface
         s   scholium

So, *E*1d7 is *Ethics*, part 1, definition 7; *E*4p37s2 is *Ethics*, part 4, proposition 37, scholium 2; *E*4p73d is *Ethics*, part 4, proposition 73, demonstration.

PT   *Political Treatise* (trans. S. Shirley, 2000)
TIE   *Treatise on the Emendation of the Intellect* (trans. E. Curley, 1985)
TTP   *Theological-Political Treatise* (trans. M. Silverthorne and J. Israel, 2007)

1

THE THEOLOGICAL-POLITICAL PROBLEM

INTRODUCTION

European society was fractured in the seventeenth century by tumultuous religious and political debates of unprecedented proportions. The debates were not over which of any number of royal heirs ought to sit on some particular throne – but over whether there should be kings and queens on thrones at all. The religious debates broadened from questions related to which Christian confession should be adopted in some particular region to the question of whether *any* religious confession should be formally adopted. The extreme emotions that these debates evoked derived from the absolutely fundamental nature of the questions being discussed. Everything was up for grabs.

As we look back on these debates from our vantage point, it is difficult to have real sympathy for the views of the majority of reasonable and law-abiding people living in Europe at this time. The right answers to the debates of the period seem so clear and obvious to us today. It seems unquestionable that each person ought

2 THE THEOLOGICAL-POLITICAL PROBLEM

to enjoy freedom of thought and expression, that democracy is the best form of political organization, and that there ought to be a separation between Church and State. But it was not always so. This book is about a philosopher Benedict (Baruch) Spinoza (1632–77), who was one of those radicals who dared to contest the regnant views about the political order and the role of religion in the State so widely accepted at the time. Spinoza was born into the Jewish community in Amsterdam, but lived most of his life apart from it. His writings on politics and religion created a firestorm of controversy in early modern Europe. His work was so controversial because Spinoza entirely rejected an approach to political thinking that had dominated Europe since roughly the fall of the Western Roman Empire. We shall call this traditional approach to politics the "Christendom Model". According to this model, the Church and the State are two independent powers that cooperate closely to forge a single workable totality out of many disparate and conflicting tribes and peoples. The ideology of the Christendom Model presumed that if the Church and the State did not actively work together, then the different tribes and nations that crisscrossed Europe could not be welded into homogeneous political units. Such heterogeneous societies would lack the internal coherence necessary for stability and peace, and so would collapse into bloody civil war. Religious uniformity was required if war was to be avoided.

In some form or other the Christendom Model dominated European political life for over a thousand years until two trends in the early modern period made it increasingly unworkable. The first trend was a dramatic rise in religious and philosophical innovation. Both the Protestant reformations and the scientific revolutions of the sixteenth and seventeenth centuries resulted in an unprecedented level of religious and scientific pluralism. The second trend was that *political* power came to be concentrated in larger and more centralized states. According to the Christendom Model, such large centralized states required a high degree of religious uniformity to maintain internal peace, but this ran against the trend of *decreasing* religious uniformity in the population. These two trends created tensions which exploded during the seventeenth century. Various wars in the name of religion were fought as different governments attempted to reconcile the Christendom

Model with the reality – and stubborn persistence – of the new religious and philosophical developments. We call the set of problems for the Christendom Model created by these two contrasting trends the "Theological-Political Problem". This complex problem centered on two related concerns:

- *The Problem of Political Legitimacy.* Without reference to religion, how is a legitimate ruler distinguished from an illegitimate one?
- *The Problem of Cooperation without Agreement.* How much peaceful cooperation is possible without deep agreement on fundamental questions?

This book is about how one brilliant and controversial philosopher, Spinoza, attempted to solve the Theological-Political Problem. Spinoza's solution involved the development of a new model of politics that we call "Liberal Republicanism". According to this view, political legitimacy cannot come from religion, but from the fact that a civil society confers on all of its citizenry positive (participatory) freedom. This positive freedom is best preserved if the State promotes institutions, including religious institutions, that inculcate the "thin" (universal and liberal) virtues of tolerance, justice, and obedience. The modern state should, therefore, retrofit existing religious institutions to aid in the cultivation of liberal republican virtues such as tolerance. If the state is successful in the cultivation of such inclusive (thin) values and norms, then the level of agreement on *fundamental* questions needed for peaceful cooperation can be greatly reduced. In this way, Spinoza boldly rejects over a thousand years of political thinking and offers in its place a comprehensive new model of politics that hopes to make possible both peace *and* pluralism at the same time.

THE CHRISTENDOM MODEL

The collapse of the Western Roman Empire in the fifth century inaugurated a period of political and social chaos. Europe would be torn apart by constant war and political uncertainty for centuries. During this chaotic time it was the Catholic Church that maintained the basic functions of everyday life in Europe. The Church

4 THE THEOLOGICAL-POLITICAL PROBLEM

handled all of the central moments of life – weddings, schooling, funerals, wills, property records, etc. – and could guarantee a modest income to its army of clergy. The Church would occupy a central role in European life for at least the next thousand years.

Given the importance of the Church in everyday life in Europe, one of the central themes in pre-modern political thought was explaining and justifying the complex web of relationships that existed between the authority of the Church and various secular political institutions. While the political thinking in the pre-modern world (by which we include both the medieval and renaissance worlds) was complex, it can be organized around a certain conception of society known as *Christendom*. According to the Christendom Model, the Church and the State are two independent powers. These powers are, however, complementary and must cooperate closely to mold a single cohesive and organic whole out of disparate social groups. As we use the term "Christendom Model" it signals not only a hope to unite the old territories of the Western Roman Empire into a single Christian commonwealth, but a view about how the Church and the State relate within any single nation or territory.

There was near universal agreement in medieval political thinking that the State needed the Church in order to survive. The Church was needed to perform at least two vital functions for secular rulers: (i) the Church helps generate, through its comprehensive pedagogical roles, a homogeneous population, which in turn binds the rulers and the ruled closely together, and (ii) the Church confers legitimacy on a ruler and his policies. Let us briefly consider each of these two critical functions in turn.

The clear importance of a close allegiance, even unity, between a resident population and its ruler immediately generates the practical consideration of how precisely that is to be achieved. The state would become unstable if the loyalty of its residents were divided between its rulers and some (extra-territorial) ethnic group with which it tended to identify. What means fostered the requisite loyalty and allegiance? On the whole, the Church, through its myriad religious institutions, was remarkably successful at creating relatively homogeneous social units across disparate tribes. After the fall of Rome, the Catholic Church was able to unify the Germanic tribes by means of converting them to its way of life. After their conversion, the disparate tribes came to accept the Church's authority over certain matters and commenced to knit larger political societies together along generally Christian lines. This success continued well into the early modern period.

The State and the political rulers also needed the Church to confer legitimacy on State authorities and policies. The power of the Church in the pre-modern period is similar in certain ways to that of the Supreme Court in the United States or to the Senate in Rome after Augustus. Lacking in real military power, the Church's main authority came from its ability to confer moral (and so political) legitimacy on a ruler or a policy. The conferral of legitimacy on a ruler is an extremely important task because without it a rival might well be emboldened to usurp authority. To take just one example, this withdrawal of legitimacy was used dramatically in the dispute between Pope Gregory VII (Hildebrand) and the Holy Roman Emperor Henry VI in 1076 when the Pope excommunicated the Emperor. In so doing the Pope formally dissolved Henry's subjects' allegiance to him. "The papal ban struck Henry with devastating effect. His supporters melted away, and his enemies used it to rally against him" (Bokenkotter 2004: 118). The Emperor was so worried about his loss of support that he famously stood for three days in the snow until the Pope finally granted absolution and readmitted him to communion. While such dramatic confrontations between the power of the papacy and the power of the State were extremely rare, the threat of a withdrawal of legitimacy in the eyes of his people was a powerful weapon in the hands of the pre-modern Popes.

THE EARLY MODERN CRISIS: RELIGIOUS INNOVATION AND POLITICAL CENTRALIZATION

Everything began to change on October 31, 1517 when Martin Luther tacked his *Ninety-Five Theses* to the Castle Church door in Wittenberg. This act would mark the symbolic beginning of an accidental revolution that would shake Europe to its foundations. A series of Protestant reformations would sweep across Europe

6 THE THEOLOGICAL-POLITICAL PROBLEM

over the next two centuries. With these reformations "the pattern of broad regional domination by one particular church [began] to disintegrate" (Israel 2006: 63). This disintegration was rapid and widespread. As Jonathan Israel writes,

> The profound spiritual crisis which ensued after 1650 was ... [partly due] to the growing fragmentation of Protestant churches themselves. For besides the three major Protestant churches, the Lutheran, Calvinist, and Anglican ... numerous dissident Protestant sects – Mennonites, Spiritualists, Socinians, Remonstrants, Quakers, and Collegiants – had arisen since the Reformation despite widespread persecution and suppression.
>
> (Israel 2006: 63)

With this fragmentation and confusion one of the central requirements of the Christendom Model of society was directly challenged. The explosion of religious sectarianism was accelerated by the reformer's call to ground one's faith exclusively on the Bible (*sola Scriptura*), as interpreted by the individual believer. The Bible was translated into many vernacular languages during this time (Luther famously translated the Bible into German), and aided with the recent invention of moveable type, the laity were encouraged to read the Bible for themselves. The Reformation expelled practices and beliefs that could find no clear warrant in Scripture. This change in the role of the Bible in Protestant Christianity had immediate and significant political implications, given the tradition of close cooperation between the Church and the State required in the Christendom Model. Within a short period of time the Bible became a revolutionary text, and divided the faithful in bloody wars. Before the Reformation the Pope himself was the primary voice of the Church, and through his alliances with the political rulers, the Church was directly involved in politics. At this time the Bible played little direct role in politics. But after the reformist movements altered the religious landscape in Europe, the Bible began to take on significant and direct political influence, with increasing destabilizing tendencies.

The new authority of the Scriptures naturally led to a flourishing of study of Holy Writ during this period. It was fashionable at

THE THEOLOGICAL-POLITICAL PROBLEM   7

this time for educated people to learn the biblical languages (not only Greek, but also Hebrew and Aramaic). Spinoza himself composed a Hebrew grammar in an effort to help some of his Protestant (and radical) friends to better familiarize themselves with the Hebrew Bible, all with a view to interpreting it in its own terms. As sectarianism advanced, the *political* implications of biblical scholarship came to the fore. A particular view on the meaning of the Scriptures thus came to have a significant impact on one's view on contemporary political questions. Biblical interpretation and politics became increasingly intertwined.

The religious innovation of the Reformation was accompanied by innovation in natural philosophy and science as well. Early modern natural philosophy was a multi-sided competition among amateur gentlemen and professionals with a dizzying array of different methodological and metaphysical presuppositions. Contemporaries often lumped these methodologies (or schools) together into what they simply called the "New Philosophy". This "New Philosophy" included at least four major and competing branches inspired by the work of key foundational figures: (1) Descartes (1596–1650), (2) Locke (1632–1704) and Newton (1643–1727), (3) Leibniz (1646–1716), and (4) Spinoza (1632–77). The first three schools constitute a part of what Jonathan Israel calls the "Moderate Enlightenment". These three schools attempted to combine traditional religious beliefs with new understandings of the natural world. In this felt need to somehow accommodate traditional religious beliefs – such as freedom of the will and divine omnipotence and omniscience – these schools may be viewed as reformist rather than revolutionary. Spinozism, by contrast, was radical and rejected traditional religion entirely (as we will see in chapter four). Not to be overlooked, and in keen competition with these new trends, there was a still powerful scholastic tradition grounded in the writings of Aquinas (1225–74). This Church tradition had its own supporters in the universities, among theologians, and among the professional classes.

Concurrent with this dizzying array of religious and scientific outlooks was a trend toward political centralization, with more centralized governments ruling ever larger and larger territories. One influential scholar of the period has concluded that

8 THE THEOLOGICAL-POLITICAL PROBLEM

> Europe had five thousand independent political units (mainly baronies and principalities) in the fifteenth century, five hundred at the time of the Thirty Years War in the early seventeenth century, two hundred at the time of Napoleon in the early nineteenth century, and fewer than thirty in 1953.
>
> (Wright 1942: 215; also Richardson 1960: 168–69; Pinker 2011: 74)

Between 1515 and 1519, for example, Charles of Habsburg acquired an empire that included "present-day Spain, the Netherlands and Belgium, parts of what is now Italy, Germany, and Austria, as well as Spain's New World possessions" (Nexon 2009: 7). The states that were created by these expanding monarchies in early modern Europe were not uniform societies with common languages, cultures, and identities. Instead, "most Europeans lived within composite states that had been cobbled together from pre-existing political units by a variety of aggressive 'princes' employing a standard repertoire of techniques including marriage, dynastic inheritance, and direct conquest" (Te Brake 1998: 14, quoted in Nexon 2009: 6).

These cobbled-together and unnatural empires were made out of pre-existing social networks and loyalties, and so created societies that were rife with internal tensions. These newly created states were "neither radically decentralized 'feudal' entities nor modern nation-states" (Nexon 2009: 6). Indeed, "many historians now use the term 'composite states' to describe the heterogeneous political communities that dominated the early modern European landscape" (Nexon *ibid.*). These fractured and heterogeneous states were always on the verge of violent dissolution.

The rise of the composite states of early modern Europe coincided with a series of religious wars. The most important of these was the Thirty Years War (1618–48), the bloodiest European conflict of the seventeenth century. This war pitted Catholic armies against Protestant armies and killed nearly a third of the population of Germany. This disastrous war came to an end in 1648 with the signing of the Peace of Westphalia. This peace treaty had at least two important aspects. First, it generally enshrined in law the territories of the composite states, such that they each included heterogeneous religions and ethnic communities. Second, it allowed each sovereign government to determine the country's religious affiliation for itself. This peace did not resolve the conflicts created by religious diversity and political consolidation, but rather enshrined them in international law. Each country would now have to resolve these complex problems within its own borders rather than on the battlefield. A new kind of political society was needed in the fragile and tense world created by the Peace of Westphalia – one that could make possible peaceful diversity.

THE THEOLOGICAL-POLITICAL PROBLEM

These two trends – increasing pluralism and increasing political centralization – and the problems they create for the Christendom Model of society are clearly on display in the political struggles in the Dutch Republic of Spinoza's time. The Dutch Republic in the seventeenth century was a collection of fiercely independent states that resisted consolidation into a single commonwealth. After the powerful royal general (called the *stadholder*) William II, Prince of Orange, died in 1650 a "Great Assembly" was called to determine whether another *stadholder* was needed to replace him. The debate that followed this assembly coalesced into two broad political and religious factions. On the one side were the "Statists" who wanted a decentralized country where most power devolved to the individual provinces. The "Statists" tended to be secular in their leanings, although they demanded a "respect for the preeminence" of the Reformed faith, and argued for a more religiously tolerant society (Nadler 2011: 45). The preeminent representative of the Statists was Johan De Witt (1625–72). De Witt rose to the office of Grand Pensionary in the 1650s following the debate after the death of William II. In the absence of a *stadholder*, he became the most important political figure in the Republic.

The Republic's second major political faction was known as the "Orangists" (after William II, Prince of Orange). This political group argued that a new *stadholder* – preferably, following tradition, from the House of Orange – should be installed in order to protect the Republic from outside invaders. This powerful head of state could then serve as a *de facto* monarch and keep the country at

10 THE THEOLOGICAL-POLITICAL PROBLEM

peace, both internally and externally. In short, this debate pitted monarchists and religious traditionalists against anti-monarchists and secularists.

Spinoza's sympathies were clearly with the Statists and he supported the decentralization of power in the Republic. His *Theological-Political Treatise* (1670) is partly a defense of the general Statist approach to politics. Nevertheless, the Statist party quickly collapsed in the Dutch Republic. The central weakness in their position was their inability to give a convincing answer to the most pressing political question of the time – how is it possible to create a pluralistic society both at peace with itself and with its neighbors? The population turned on the De Witt brothers (and killed them brutally in 1672) when it became clear that the decentralization of power and acceptance of religious diversity left them vulnerable to invasion and conquest, especially from the French.

Written within this political environment, Spinoza's works seem to have two related audiences. First, there is an audience of educated citizens of the Dutch Republic, current with recent trends in science and philosophy. This appears to be the most immediate audience that Spinoza has in view. But the issues he raises and the questions he attempts to answer transcend the particularities of the Dutch situation and touch on the fundamental political problem of the age – how to modify or replace the Christendom Model in light of the two divergent trends that were tearing it apart. As we have noted, these are:

- *The Problem of Political Legitimacy*: Without reference to religion, how is a legitimate ruler distinguished from an illegitimate one?
- *The Problem of Cooperation without Agreement*: How much peaceful cooperation is possible without deep agreement on fundamental questions?

These are the two problems that were at the heart of the constant turmoil in early modern Europe. Attempts to answer these questions eventually led Spinoza to a secular, democratic, and liberal theory of the state. But in Spinoza's day this was by no means the obviously correct choice. In order to transition from the Christendom Model to the Liberal Republican Model a lot of theoretical work had to be done to show that such a society could function and would not tear itself apart in a bloody civil war.

The remainder of this book examines this transition from the Christendom Model to the Liberal Republican Model. As we shall see, this move requires reconsidering the relationship between natural right and the natural law (chapter two); the pre-political state of humankind and how political power can be morally justified (chapter three); the problems with founding politics on traditional biblical religion (chapter four); the ways that religion can be revised to help create a peaceful and pluralistic society (chapter five); the role and importance of toleration in a peaceful and pluralistic society (chapter six); and finally the nature and viability of democracy, and the role of virtue in public life (chapter seven). It is our view that Spinoza provides an innovative and comprehensive solution to the central political and religious problems facing early modern Europe. He is the first important author to argue strenuously for a secular, liberal, and democratic state.

CONCLUSION

This chapter has in brief provided a context and a starting point for the study of Spinoza's political philosophizing. We have noted the tremendous staying power and appeal of the Christendom Model of society, whereby Church and State cooperate closely and inter-actively to create a single organic and unified political society. In the early modern period, however, two trends made this model untenable. First, there was a significant increase in religious and scientific pluralism following the Protestant reformations and the new scientific movements that swept across Europe. Second, political power began to coalesce around a few centralized monarchs who ruled over larger and more internally diverse populations. According to the Christendom Model, this concentration of power required a high degree of religious uniformity, but this requirement came at just the time when such uniformity was practically impossible. Thus, Europe was engaged in nearly continuous religious warfare for the hundred years preceding the Peace of Westphalia in 1648. In the tense peace that followed the signing of this treaty each state had to find a way to rule over increasingly diverse religious populations. The peace was a fragile one and many worried that any spark could set the whole continent ablaze once again. It is in this tense political and religious environment that Spinoza wrote.

FURTHER READING

Among recent studies of this time period in European history, the most comprehensive are Israel (2001) and (2006). For a detailed study of the Dutch Republic in the seventeenth century, see Prak (2005). Helpful introductions to the contemporary context of Spinoza's politics can be found in Nadler (2011, chapters 1–3) and James (2012, Introduction and chapter one). The standard biography of Spinoza in English is Nadler (1999).

2

NATURALISM, RIGHT, AND POWER

INTRODUCTION

One of the most infamous and important claims in Spinoza's political writings is his claim that "the right of each thing extends so far as its determined power extends" (*Theological-Political Treatise* [hereafter *TTP*] 16.2). Spinoza claims that right and power are coextensive. Notice, however, that Spinoza does not claim that right and power are *identical*. He simply claims that the scope of one's natural right extends exactly as far as one's power does, and it does not follow from this claim that one's natural right simply *is* one's power, whatever exactly that might mean. We call the thesis that natural right and power are coextensive the "Natural Rights Thesis". Many commentators take the Natural Rights Thesis to entail that "might makes right". This interpretation is a natural one on first reading, but it is mistaken. If Spinoza did believe that might makes right, then he would be committed to believing that anything the State actually succeeds in doing must be right. We find the prospect of attributing such a view to Spinoza – as old as Thrasymachus in Plato's *Republic* – implausible. One major

14 NATURALISM, RIGHT, AND POWER

problem with this view is that the *Theological-Political Treatise* is full of criticisms of existing power structures. For example, Spinoza argues that religious leaders should not dictate public policy and that governments should secure unlimited freedom of conscience. Reading Spinoza as a diehard supporter of the regnant norms is at odds with much of the *Theological-Political Treatise*. We conclude, therefore, that Spinoza rejects the claim that "might makes right". To make sense of Spinoza's political philosophy, we must begin by examining what exactly the Natural Rights Thesis does mean.

In this chapter we argue that the Natural Rights Thesis should be interpreted as a rejection of the natural law tradition, as Spinoza understood it. Spinoza is rejecting the claim that there exists an *external and transcendent* moral standard to which human behavior and human society must conform. For Spinoza, one has the natural right to do whatever one has the power to do, in the sense that one's actions cannot violate some external and transcendent moral law that is imposed from above, simply because no such law exists.

To argue for this interpretation we begin with an examination of the concepts of *power* and *natural right* in Spinoza. We contrast Spinoza's conception of natural right with those of Hobbes and Locke, which *prima facie* bear strong comparison. Having clarified these essential concepts, we then distinguish three different kinds of *law*: laws of nature, natural laws, and positive laws. We then argue that Spinoza's commitment to *Naturalism*, the view that everything in nature, including human beings, is governed by the same set of general laws, entails the rejection of natural law (and the natural law tradition), because the latter applies only to human beings and not to nature as a whole.

We end this chapter by examining one of the most contentious questions in the literature on Spinoza's moral and political philosophy: the question of whether Spinoza offers a *normative* political theory or merely a *descriptive* one. We argue that Spinoza's political theory is *weakly normative*, and by this we mean that, while Spinoza prescribes to governments what they *should* do, he claims they cannot be blameworthy (in any robust moral sense) for failing to do what they should. Reading Spinoza's political theory as weakly normative stands as a defensible compromise between a strongly normative theory and a merely descriptive one.

POWER AND NATURAL RIGHT

Spinoza argues in the *Ethics* that "each thing, insofar as it is in itself [*quantum in se est*], strives to persevere in its own being" (*E*3p6). This striving constitutes the *essence* of each thing (*E*3p7), and Spinoza uses the term *power* as a general term to indicate how successfully a thing strives to persevere in its own being. The more successfully something strives, the healthier and more vital it is, and so the more *power* it possesses. A person who strives successfully is able to do more of the things that are required in order to survive and so Spinoza would say that the agent has more power.

Spinoza further argues that each thing that exists is always and at all times doing whatever it can do to survive. Nothing ever destroys itself (*E*3p4). In fact, Spinoza believes self-destruction and suicide are conceptually incoherent and logically impossible. If something is destroyed, it is *always* caused to be destroyed by something *outside* of itself. Self-destruction is impossible. Spinoza conceives of the whole of nature (not just plants and animals) as engaging in a giant struggle for existence, with each natural organism behaving in such a way that it becomes as powerful as it can, given the pressures from external things upon it. The more powerful something is, the better able it is to ward off external forces and so save itself from destruction, at least temporarily. So *power* in Spinoza is defined as the ability to survive in the universal struggle for continued existence. We might note as an aside here that this is not the only point where a comparison between Spinoza and Nietzsche, who expressed great admiration for Spinoza, may be discerned.

Spinoza claims in the Natural Rights Thesis that the extent of one's power is the same as the extent of one's natural right (*TTP* 16.2). But what does he mean by *natural right*? A right is some sort of freedom or liberty to do something. There are two general conceptions of natural right in early modern political theory: *liberty rights* and *claim rights*. The conceptual difference between these two hinges on a notion of obligation and restraint, whether or not an individual stands under an obligation not to interfere with the exercise of another's rights. One has a *liberty right* to do x when one has the right to do x and other people also have the right to interfere with one's doing of x. For example, we all have a *liberty*

16 NATURALISM, RIGHT, AND POWER

right to compete in a fair contest. Your liberty right to compete in the competition does not put me under an obligation to avoid entering the competition. I too have a liberty right to enter the competition and so, perhaps, take the prize from you. By contrast, one has a *claim right* to do x when one has the right to do x and this right puts all others under an obligation *not* to interfere with one's doing of x. For example, I have a *claim right* to my car. I own my car and this puts all others under an obligation (at least under normal circumstances) not to use my car without my permission. Ownership of something is usually taken to include certain claim rights. Famously, Hobbes argued that without a sovereign there exist only liberty rights (*Leviathan* 1.13, 2.21). In a state of nature there exists no ownership of property, but merely (temporary) possession of it. The sovereign's laws (backed up by the threat of force) bring claim rights, and ownership of property, into existence. Locke, on the other hand, argued that certain claim rights are instituted by God, and so exist even without a sovereign to enforce them. Locke argued further that everyone has the "executive authority" to enforce these claim rights by punishing violators (*Second Treatise on Government* 2.6–7). According to Locke, these claim rights constitute a "natural law" which can be rationally deduced by all human beings. We will discuss this claim further in the next section.

When Spinoza claims that natural rights are coextensive with power (one's ability to help oneself in the struggle for continued existence), is he referring to claim rights or liberty rights? It is clear that Spinoza intends that it is liberty rights that extend as far as one's power. Spinoza writes that:

> Anyone therefore deemed to be under the government of nature alone [i.e., in an area without any successful political authority] is permitted by the sovereign right of nature to desire anything that he believes to be useful to himself, whether brought to this by sound reason or by the impulse of his passions. He is permitted to take it for himself by any means – by force, by fraud, by pleading – whatever will most easily enable him to obtain it, and thus he is permitted to regard as an enemy anyone who tries to prevent his getting his way.

> *(TTP* 16.3)

It is clear from this passage that the one who takes another person's possessions (before a sovereign has been constituted) does not violate any claim right of that person. The same would go for one's life, activities, and organizations. According to Spinoza, nothing one does creates claim rights to anything – including one's own life! – prior to the existence of a sovereign power.

We are now able to clarify what the Natural Rights Thesis says. Spinoza is claiming that *one's ability to survive in the struggle for existence is coextensive with a liberty right to do anything believed to be useful in that struggle*. One has the right to do whatever one thinks must be done in order to survive (and others have the right to interfere if they want). It is important to note how different this claim is from the claim that "might makes right". The Natural Rights Thesis is actually inconsistent with the claim that "might makes right" because the power of one person never creates any kind of *obligation* for others to obey. Rather, everyone always has the liberty right to do whatever one believes will help in the struggle to survive. Cooperation with a powerful person or group may sometimes (perhaps often) appear to be in one's best interest, but acquiescence to the power structure cannot be made *obligatory* by the mere fact that the power structure is powerful. Might does not in itself make right. On this view Spinoza and Hobbes (at least the Hobbes of the *Leviathan*) are in substantial agreement.

NATURAL LAWS, POSITIVE LAWS, AND LAWS OF NATURE

Before we consider further Spinoza's argument for the Natural Rights Thesis, it is important to distinguish three different kinds of law: laws of nature, natural laws, and positive laws. The laws of nature are *descriptive* laws that govern the movement of all physical objects and, according to Spinoza, the sequence of all thoughts, which he believes to be as causally determined as bodies. Spinoza believes that every movement of every physical object and every sequence of thoughts is fully determined by the past and the laws of nature.

The laws of nature should not be confused with *prescriptive* natural laws. The latter are normative, they are about how we *ought* to act. These laws are binding on human beings, but are not

18 NATURALISM, RIGHT, AND POWER

instituted by human beings. Such natural laws are sometimes parsed as the "moral law" and are often seen as governing practical reason. The history of natural law theory is complex and the term "natural law" is applied in many contexts (both legal and moral), which in fact have very little in common with one another. Nevertheless, we can distinguish two general strands of natural law theory relevant to our purposes here: theistic natural law theory and non-theistic natural law theory.

Theistic natural law theory is summed up famously by Richard Hooker (d. 1600), who asserts that "the laws of nature do bind men absolutely, even as they are men, although they have never any settled fellowship" (*Of the Laws of Ecclesiastical Polity* 1.10). These laws come directly from God who enforces them by administering punishments for violators. Those who do not follow these laws are morally blameworthy for not doing so and are punished by God accordingly. On this traditional reading, natural laws are simply positive laws instituted and enforced by God. Obeying these laws is necessary for human beings to fulfill their purpose or end (*telos*) as a human being and achieve ultimate union with God. According to Hooker, when one violates one of these God-given decrees of the natural law, one acts wrongly, even if one is outside of civil society. These laws are discovered by the consideration of our nature. Aquinas argues that "the rule and measure of human acts is reason, which is the first principle of human acts" (*Summa Theologiae* I–II, q. 90, I). Because our practical reason is given to us by God, our reason tells us what the natural laws prescribed by God are. Nevertheless, these natural laws are not binding on us because they derive from human reason, but rather because they come from God. God the lawgiver makes the natural laws binding. He reveals them to us by means of practical reason. On the theistic view, without God the natural law creates no obligation to obey it.

The second strand of natural law theory is non-theistic natural law theory. This strand can be found most prominently in the works of Grotius and Hobbes. By contrast to Hooker and Aquinas, they argue that practical reason *by itself* can reveal prescriptive rules that we must follow in order to achieve our ends. Hobbes argues that each person seeks self-preservation. The Hobbesian natural laws are the different prescriptions that need to be followed in order to guarantee such self-preservation; for example, one must be willing to give up one's natural right to all things if others are likewise inclined. In this telling of non-theistic natural law theory, these laws are binding on us even if they are not underwritten by divine or human sanctions. In Grotius's famous passage, he argues that

> What we have been saying [about the natural laws] would have a degree of validity even if we should concede that which cannot be conceded without the utmost wickedness, that there is no God, or that the affairs of men are of no concern to him.
>
> (*Prolegomena to the War of Law and Peace*, sec. 11)

According to non-theistic natural law theory, God may perhaps reveal to human beings what the natural law is, but these laws are binding whether or not God exists, or underwrites the laws with punishments. Non-theistic natural law theory is "non-theistic" not in the sense that it requires God's non-existence, but only in the sense that the natural law does not depend upon God for its obligatory force.

Non-theistic natural law theory has a complicated connection with moral philosophy. While some non-theistic natural law theorists, including Hobbes himself in *De Cive*, claim that the natural law just is the moral law, and obligates as such, one must understand that the natural laws of Hobbes do not have the kind of deontic, obligatory force that, for example, Kantian imperatives have; rather they must be understood as prudential rules for joint survival. Natural laws are simply prudential means to contingent, but perhaps often desired, ends. If one gives up the end (such as peace, security, survival), then one is no longer obligated to follow the laws. Natural laws understood in this way are what Kant would later call prudential *hypothetical imperatives*. They are of the following form: *If you desire x, then do y*. If one does not desire x, then one is in no way obligated to do y. Thus, natural law y binds the agent contingently, if and only if he desires and aims at x.

We may further distinguish two different strands of non-theistic natural law theory: moralistic and amoralistic. The difference between them concerns whether or not the non-theistic natural

20 NATURALISM, RIGHT, AND POWER

law has the obligatory and censorious force of moral laws. Thus, there are two different claims made by non-theistic natural law theorists:

(i)   There are rationally known rules that make possible joint survival, even if there is no God.
(ii) We are morally blameworthy if we do not follow these rules.

The moralistic natural law theorists accept both (i) and (ii) and the amoralistic natural law theorists accept only (i). It is important to note that the amoralistic natural law theorists are not necessarily committed to believing that there are no moral laws binding on human beings. These theorists are only committed to claiming that such moral laws are something other than the prescriptive rational rules for joint survival.

The third kind of law, in addition to the laws of nature and natural laws, is positive law. This is law established by a sovereign power and backed up with threats of punishment. When a government enacts a law that we should all drive on the right side of the road, this law is a positive law, underwritten with penalties and subject to change. Positive laws can change in a way that neither laws of nature nor natural laws can.

Having cleared up the conceptual landscape, let us now return to Spinoza's own views. Spinoza clearly believes that there are universal laws of nature and that there are (human-made) positive laws. Further, Spinoza rules out any conceptual space for *theistic* natural law theory – God does not create positive laws. Positive laws are created by human beings. But what is his understanding of *non-theistic* natural laws, the rationally known rules which make possible joint survival? Is his view "moralistic" or "amoralistic"? Is Spinoza committed to claims (i) and (ii) above, or just (i)?

At the opening of chapter four of the *Theological-Political Treatise*, Spinoza writes:

> The word law (*lex*) in an absolute sense signifies that, in accordance with which, each individual thing, or all things, or all things of a same kind, behave in one and the same fixed and determined way, depending upon either natural necessity or a human decision. A law

that depends upon natural necessity is one that necessarily follows from the very nature or definition of a thing. A law that depends upon a human decision, which is more properly called a decree (*jus*), is one that men prescribe to themselves and to others in order to achieve a better and safer life ...

(*TTP* 4.1)

In this passage Spinoza is clear that the only laws that exist are the ones that either follow from the nature of the thing or those that are instituted by human beings. In fact, Spinoza is reluctant to call a positive law a "law" (*lex*) because positive laws do not hold for everything in nature, but only for some natural beings, namely, human beings inhabiting a particular civil society. For Spinoza, a positive law is not a *law*, but it is rather a *decree* (*jus*). Properly speaking, the only laws that exist are the laws that follow directly from the nature or definition of a thing; in fact, these laws follow from even more basic facts about the nature of the universe (see the "physical digression" following *E*2p13).

Once again, the overarching question is Spinoza's understanding of *non-theistic* natural laws, the laws binding on us as the particular kind of natural being we are. Are such laws (merely) descriptive laws – rational rules that make possible joint survival without any moral, censorious force – or are they prescriptive rational laws – natural laws with the obligatory force of moral laws? Spinoza's causal determinism guarantees that knowing the nature of a thing will certainly tell us how it will – indeed must – behave. But can the nature of a thing tell us how it *should* behave? This question is a difficult one and we cannot fully answer it at this point. Instead we will put this question to one side and return to it at the end of this chapter. There we will argue that prescriptive rational laws do indeed follow from the nature of a thing, but that these laws do not have the obligatory force of moral laws.

NATURALISM AND THE NATURAL RIGHTS THESIS

We have now cleared the conceptual space to approach the argument for Spinoza's Natural Rights Thesis. As a reminder, we interpret this thesis as claiming that *one's ability to survive in the struggle for*

22 NATURALISM, RIGHT, AND POWER

existence is coextensive with a liberty right to do anything believed to be useful in that struggle. Spinoza provides only one explicit argument for this claim. We call this argument the Divine Natural Right Argument. This argument is presented in both the *Theological-Political Treatise* and the *Political Treatise*. The argument in the *Theological-Political Treatise* is:

> It is certain that nature, considered wholly in itself, has a sovereign right to do everything that it can do, i.e., the right of nature extends as far as its power extends. For the power of nature is the very power of God who has supreme right to [do] all things. However, since the universal power of the whole of nature is nothing but the power of all individual things together, it follows that each individual thing has the sovereign right to do everything that it can do, or the right of each thing extends as far as its determined power extends.
>
> *(TTP* 16.2)

He makes the same argument again in the *Political Treatise* {hereafter *PT*]:

> From the fact that the power of natural things by which they exist and act is the very power of God, we can readily understand what is the right of Nature. Since God has right over all things, and God's right is nothing other than God's power in so far as that is considered as absolutely free, it follows that every natural thing has as much right from Nature as it has power to exist and to act. For the power of every natural thing by which it exists and acts is nothing other than the power of God, which is absolutely free.
>
> *(PT* 2.3)

The argument that Spinoza presents here seems to be roughly as follows:

(1) Everything that is done from God's power is done by right. (Premise 1)
(2) The power of Nature is the power of God. (Premise 2)
(3) Thus, everything done by the power of Nature is done by right. (From 1, 2)

(4) Everything humans do, they do from the power of Nature (or God). (Premise 3)
(5) Thus, everything humans do, they do by right. (From 3, 4)

This argument for Spinoza's Natural Rights Thesis is grounded in his general commitment to "naturalism". By "naturalism" we mean the thesis that everything in nature is governed by the same set of general laws. There are not different laws governing the behavior of rocks, plants, animals, and human beings, respectively. Rather there is only one set of basic laws governing all of nature. "The way of understanding the nature of anything, of whatever kind," Spinoza writes, "must also be the same, viz. through the universal laws and rules of Nature" (*E*3 pref.). Human beings, as Spinoza famously says, are not privileged – they are not a "kingdom within a kingdom" (*E*3 pref.).

This rejection of the domain-restricted preeminence of human beings has a radical effect on Spinoza's conception of politics and society. Naturalism entails that we must analyze human beings as embedded in nature and subject to her laws, and not in a manner that presumes that human beings are "outside" of nature and so exempt from the laws that govern everything else. The Natural Rights Thesis holds throughout all of nature. For humans no less than for a pack of wild animals, their natural right, grounded ultimately in the universality of the laws of nature (and divine power), extends as far as their determined power extends.

There seems to be nothing unusual about claiming that the Natural Rights Thesis holds for wild animals. Spinoza's radical move is to apply this thesis to human beings. When it comes to non-rational animals it is reasonable to claim that they have a right to do whatever it is in their power to do. When a dog kills a cat there is no objection based on the claim that the dog has violated the cat's right to live or some such. The dog, it is reasonable to believe, has a natural right to kill the cat because it has the power to do so. The Natural Rights Thesis holds for dogs. Spinoza's commitment to naturalism, however, rules out the possibility that natural right is coextensive with power *for only some beings (like dogs) but not others (like humans)*. There can be no law that binds *only* on human beings. Such a limiting (moralistic) law would place certain

24 NATURALISM, RIGHT, AND POWER

activities "outside" a human being's natural right that are *nevertheless* within her power (murder, theft, rape, etc.). But if such were the case for humans, then given naturalism, it would be true for everything in nature as well (e.g., animals, plants, and even rocks). But such a result is surely absurd. It is hard to see what it would mean exactly to claim that plants and rocks were violating moral laws. Thus, it seems that a commitment to Spinozistic naturalism entails a commitment to the Natural Rights Thesis. We can formalize this argument from naturalism to the Natural Rights Thesis as follows:

(1) The whole of nature is bound by one and the same set of laws. (Premise 1)
(2) Suppose that a moralistic natural law exists that is binding only on human beings. (Premise 2, for *reductio*)
(3) This moralistic natural law shrinks the scope of the natural right (only) of human beings so that their natural right is no longer coextensive with their determined power. (Premise 3)
(4) Human beings make up only part of nature. (Premise 4)
(5) Thus, there exist some laws (namely, the moralistic natural laws) that bind on only part of nature, but not on the whole. (From 2, 4)
(6) But (1) and (5) are in contradiction
(7) Thus, Premise 2 is false.

If one is committed to this kind of naturalism, then it is impossible to shrink the scope of the natural right of human beings without doing so for the whole of nature. A Spinozistic naturalist would have to choose between constraining the natural rights of all things in nature, or constraining the natural rights of none of them. Spinoza goes for the second option. Given this choice, Spinoza rejects all forms of *moralistic* natural law theory rather than accept the absurdity of holding trees and rocks to moral account.

SPINOZA'S WEAKLY NORMATIVE POLITICAL THEORY

Spinoza's naturalism entails that it is incoherent to censure a human being for his behavior in the sense that we hold him

NATURALISM, RIGHT, AND POWER **25**

accountable to an "extra-natural" standard, a norm that stands outside of Nature. Nevertheless, it is a fact that we do blame or censure one another. When I hear about a grizzly murder, I instinctively *blame* the killer for having done such a terrible thing. What can this mean if Spinoza's naturalism is correct? In the *Ethics* Spinoza answers this question by giving a "weakly normative" account of censure/blame (*vituperium*). He argues that blame is simply pain accompanied by the idea of an action (E3p29s). Given the Natural Rights Thesis, this is the only sense that we can make of "moral censure" in a Spinozistic universe. When my dog gets loose and kills a cat, I can censure or blame him only in the sense that I feel pain when I think about his action. Similarly, if a tree falls on my car, the only sense in which I can censure or blame the tree is that I feel pain when I think about what happened. For Spinoza, the behavior and actions of human beings is as determined as the behavior of dogs, and the behavior of dogs is as determined as the behavior of trees and rocks. For Spinoza, one can no more hold a human being blameworthy than we can a dog or a tree. Now we may (mistakenly) believe, of course, that human beings have free will to act or not to act in a given way. Thus, we may (mistakenly) believe that the killer could have chosen not to do the grizzly murder. But Spinoza argues clearly in the *Appendix* to Part I of the *Ethics* that any such conception of free will is entirely illusory. If a man commits a grizzly murder, then it could not *not* have happened. Thus, it is impossible to *blame* him in the way we would normally use the term, but it does make sense to feel pain when we think of his action. We can blame him only in this sense.

This conclusion seems to entail the impossibility of normative political theory. If blameworthiness and moral culpability are unjustifiable, then it seems as though Spinoza can do no more than provide us with a *descriptive* theory of political life, offering no more than data on how human beings actually behave. It seems that Spinoza cannot offer us any advice or proffer suggestions as to how we *ought* to behave. While this conclusion appears unavoidable, it does not follow. To see why, consider the following two theses:

> *Prescriptive Thesis*: There are norms such that if human beings followed them they would benefit.

Evaluation Thesis: There are norms for which human beings are blameworthy for not following.

We call a theory *strongly normative* if it accepts both the Prescriptive Thesis and the Evaluation Thesis. Such a theory has norms that benefit human beings and for which one is blameworthy for not following. We call a theory *weakly normative* if it accepts only the Prescriptive Thesis, but not the Evaluation Thesis. According to such a theory, it makes sense to suggest what human beings ought to do (namely, what would benefit them), but it does not make sense to censure them for failing to do so. In our view, Spinoza's political theory is weakly normative in this sense. Weak normativity is clearest in cases where we are evaluating non-rational animal groups. In these cases we can recognize when the group as a whole or some member of the group is making a mistake. It is not doing what is in its own objective best interests. It is doing what in this sense it should not do. If we can, we should step in and stop the behavior for the good of the group. Nevertheless, it makes no sense to blame or criticize the animals (except in Spinoza's extremely weak naturalistic sense examined above). For Spinoza, it is no different for human beings, who *should* act in certain ways that are beneficial, but are not, indeed cannot be, *obligated* to do so. In our view the debate concerning whether Spinoza's political theory is normative or descriptive largely presupposes a false dichotomy. The debate concerns only the question of whether his theory is what we call strongly normative or merely descriptive. Once the Prescriptive Thesis is distinguished from the Evaluation Thesis, however, it becomes possible to cut a path between these two interpretations. Indeed, as we shall see in the context of our discussion of Spinoza's critique of traditional religion in our chapter four, weak normativity is at work in his revisionist discussion of the divine laws in chapter four of the *Theological-Political Treatise*. Spinoza argues there, perhaps surprisingly, that the divine law is actually *human* law that aims at the highest good (*TTP* 4.6). In so reconceiving the divine law, Spinoza is able to comprehend the entirety of the social and political life of human beings within the scope of his naturalism.

CONCLUSION

Let us return to our foundational question in this chapter. Does Spinoza accept that "might makes right"? The answer is clearly no, if we interpret this thesis as claiming that "whatever a government does is in its own best interest" or as claiming "we ought not to interfere with the activities of any existing government under any circumstances." Spinoza rejects this kind of radical status-quo conservatism. Spinoza claims only that in the universal struggle for existence, everything has a liberty right to do whatever seems to it to be in its own best interest. No action can violate a moralistic natural law because no such law exists. No such law exists because such a law would apply only to parts of the natural world in violation of Spinoza's principled naturalism. An action may be incorrect or irrational only insofar as it may not yield the best results for the agent.

FURTHER READING

For Spinoza's rejection of the natural law tradition, see Curley (1991) and A. Garrett (2003); for a contrasting view of Spinoza as some kind of natural law theorist, see Miller (2012). For the coextensivity of right and power ("might makes right") in Spinoza, see Curley (1996). For a classic and influential analysis of Spinoza's conception of normativity, see Curley (1973). D. Garrett (1996) and LeBuffe (2010) also discuss Spinoza's moral theory and understanding of good and bad. For some relevant comparisons and contrasts between Hobbes and Spinoza on rights and power, see D. Garrett (2010), Malcolm (1991), and Curley (1992).

3

THE STATE OF NATURE AND THE ORIGINS OF CIVIL SOCIETY

INTRODUCTION

In this chapter we examine three related issues: Spinoza's account of the state of nature, why people in a state of nature would want to leave this state by forming a civil society, and how people in a state of nature actually come together and form a civil society. Our focus is on the distinctiveness of Spinoza's views on the state of nature and social contract theory. The state of nature (an arena without any political authority) and the social contract do not play the roles in Spinoza's political philosophy that they play in the more familiar theories of Hobbes, Locke, or even Rousseau. While these theorists disagree among themselves about many things, the general structure of their theories is similar. The pre-political state of nature, according to these classical theorists, is a state of natural freedom, wherein one is beholden to nobody but oneself. This natural freedom is a natural right. Setting up a political authority restricts this natural freedom and so requires a justification. The social contract is meant to provide this justification for

THE STATE OF NATURE AND THE ORIGINS OF CIVIL SOCIETY   **29**

the limitation of natural freedom that comes with the creation of a political authority. This general model of the state of nature and social contract is what we call the "classical model." We argue in this chapter that Spinoza's views on the state of nature and social contract theory do not follow this classical model.

The key difference between Spinoza and the classical social contract theorists is their differing conceptions of freedom. Spinoza does not conceive of the state of nature as a state of freedom, but as one of slavery. Freedom is possible only in the context of civil society. Given that the move from a state of nature to civil society is a move from slavery to freedom, this move does not require the kind of justification that the classical social contract theorists offer. As Spinoza claims in his letter to Jarig Jellis on June 2, 1674, "[a]s regards political theories, the difference which you inquire about between Hobbes and myself consists in this, that I always pre-serve natural right intact ..." Once the slave (the human being in a state of nature) is freed, the slave has certainly not *lost* any of his natural rights. Spinoza's understanding of the state of nature and his social contract theory can, therefore, be read as an *inversion* of the classical model.

We begin this chapter with a very broad outline of classical social contract theory. We then examine Spinoza's distinctive views on freedom and bondage and why civil society is necessary for individual freedom. Finally, we close with an examination of how Spinoza's social contract theory provides a "weakly normative" justification of political authority.

CLASSICAL SOCIAL CONTRACT THEORY

We commence with a straightforward and simple sketch relating the state of nature, the social contract, and civil society in classical social contract theory. Not surprisingly there is much discussion in the scholarly literature over how best to read Hobbes, Locke, and Rousseau on issues such as the precise nature of the social contract (is it an actual or merely hypothetical contract?), but we will pass over issues such as these because we wish to focus on a fundamental disagreement that Spinoza has with all of these thinkers. According to the classical model, the story commences with the

30 THE STATE OF NATURE AND THE ORIGINS OF CIVIL SOCIETY

pre-political state of nature, a "state" without government or political authority. This state of nature has no laws, no police, no courts, no kings, etc. Without such constraining mechanisms this state is one of natural freedom to do as one wishes without political interference. This natural freedom, however, entails insecurity. For Hobbes, the state of nature is gripped by fear. Life in the state of nature is, as he famously declares, "solitary, poor, nasty, brutish, and short" (*Leviathan* 1.13.9). In such a state there exists no possibility for the kind of complex cooperation and human interactions that would make possible any sort of cultural endeavors such as literature, art, and music. According to Hobbes and Locke, this state of nature is intolerable.

The inhabitants of the state of nature need to coalesce and form a civil association. They invest someone (or some group) with *political* authority, the authority to create laws and the power to punish those who do not follow them. These laws and the power that underwrites them establish the security and predictability necessary for human cooperation and survival. This political authority perforce has the power to limit each person's natural freedom. It is in fact the only person (or group of persons) that possesses the authority and power to use force to maintain order. Such a dispensation limits each individual's natural right.

Since the creation of a political authority limits each individual's natural right, there needs to be, on the classical model, a *justification* for this constraining mechanism. What grounds the authority of the State and its power to enforce its laws by sanction and punishment? According to the classical model, the social contract is the justification for the State's authority. The social contract is generated out of the insecurity and violence (whether real or imagined) in the state of nature. Each individual in the state of nature assents to give up some of his natural freedom in order to gain the security and other benefits that the political state provides. The political authority that is then brought into being is legitimated precisely because its existence depends on some sort of consent or agreement of those over whom it rules. This contractual obligation provides the State with legitimacy because the State in making and upholding laws is doing nothing other than what the original contractors (and, according to Locke, what their contemporary descendants)

THE STATE OF NATURE AND THE ORIGINS OF CIVIL SOCIETY   31

demanded. When the State limits natural freedoms, it is not in violation of an individual's natural rights since these latter have been voluntarily alienated.

The classical model of the relationship between the state of nature, the social contract, and civil society is relatively straightforward, even psychologically compelling. To be sure, it raises ongoing questions about the limits and scope of the contractual agreement, the methods of enforcing it, and the optimal form and constitution of the political authority. As important as these questions are within the classical social contract model, Spinoza approaches these issues in an entirely different way. The need for a justification of political authority by means of a contractual obligation that we note in the classical theorists simply does not exist for Spinoza. His naturalism, which we have previously discussed, militates against the strong normative thrust of the classical theorists. We recall that, for Spinoza, natural right is coextensive with power. As a result, once the sovereign political authority comes to possess the power to promulgate and enforce laws, it has the *right* to do so. No additional justification for consent is required to grant the sovereign this right, for simple obedience is sufficient (*TTP* 20.8). But the most important reason for the divergence of Spinoza's political theorizing from those of the classical theorists is his clear and absolute rejection of the classical (specifically, Hobbes') conception of freedom, and his rejection of the idea of the state of nature as a state of maximal freedom. This (Hobbesian) notion of natural freedom is understood as freedom from interference, so-called "negative freedom". For the classical contract theorists, freedom is the starting point in the story of the (political) progression to security and away from the insecurity inherent in the state of nature. In the place of this (negative) freedom, Spinoza offers what we call "rational freedom". On this view, freedom is *not* non-interference, but rather obedience to reason and freedom from determination by the passions. On this model one is not un-free (enslaved) by virtue of the power of external political authorities, but rather by being in the thrall of one's own passions. Given this conception, the state of nature is not a state of freedom, but rather one of bondage to fear and even superstition. For Spinoza, one is free only when one is living in a safe civil society, free from fear and superstition, and under the rule of reason. For

32 THE STATE OF NATURE AND THE ORIGINS OF CIVIL SOCIETY

Spinoza, freedom and authority are not in opposition. This revision in the idea of freedom undermines the classical social contract theorist's project of legitimating and providing justification for political authority. There is no need for justification for freeing *slaves*. They give up nothing of value. As Spinoza's conception of rational freedom is essential to his political philosophy, we pause to examine this crucial idea.

FREEDOM AND BONDAGE

Spinoza discusses freedom in all of his major works: the *Treatise on the Emendation of the Intellect*, the *Short Treatise on God, Man, and His Well-Being*, the *Theological-Political Treatise*, the *Ethics*, and the *Political Treatise*. The correct understanding of freedom and its importance to both moral and political philosophy is a central concern of Spinoza throughout his career. The *Ethics*, his last complete and greatest work, concludes with a discussion of human freedom. One difficulty students often encounter when approaching Spinoza's views on freedom is that while Spinoza does believe in human freedom, he does not believe that humans have free will. Spinoza argues in the *Ethics* that "in nature there is nothing contingent, but all things have been determined from the necessity of the divine nature to exist and produce an effect in a certain way" (*E*1p29). In the *Appendix* to Part I of the *Ethics*, Spinoza draws the explicit inference that free will does not exist. Spinoza writes:

> Men think themselves free, because they are conscious of their volitions and their appetite, and do not think, even in their dreams, of the causes by which they are disposed to wanting and willing, because they are ignorant of [those causes].

If human beings were aware of those causes, they would no longer believe that they have the power to choose or not to choose by exercising their "free will". We think we have free will only because of our ignorance of the nature of reality.

While free will is an illusion, Spinoza nevertheless believes that human *freedom* exists. Spinoza defines freedom at the beginning of *Ethics* Part I. He writes that a "thing is called free which exists

THE STATE OF NATURE AND THE ORIGINS OF CIVIL SOCIETY   33

from the necessity of its nature alone, and is determined to act by itself alone" (*E*1d7). For Spinoza, there is only one thing which exists and acts from the necessity of its nature alone – the one infinite substance (God). Nevertheless, human beings are capable of varying degrees of freedom, and more or less freedom is dependent upon whether one's own particular nature is determining one's actions or whether one's actions are determined by external causes. Spinoza makes this point in the *Political Treatise*, where he writes that:

> I call a man altogether free in so far as he is guided by reason, because it is to that extent that he is determined to action by causes that can be adequately understood solely through his own nature, even though he is necessarily determined to action by these causes. For freedom ... does not remove the necessity of the action, but imposes it.

> (*PT* 2.11)

For our purposes, there are two interesting points in this passage. First, Spinoza claims that one is free only when one's nature determines one's actions. Second, he claims that a human being is most determined by his nature when he is acting from reason. Spinoza conceives of rationality as a kind of activity, an active engagement of the mind. The more the mind is being determined by its own (rational) nature and not by the nature of things outside of it, the more active and the less passive and dependent it is. Freedom is a function of rational excellence for Spinoza. He says elsewhere in the *Political Treatise* that "freedom, in fact, is virtue or perfection; so anything that signifies weakness in man cannot be referred to his freedom" (*PT* 2.7). The more virtuous or perfect (or rational) a person is, the less he is enslaved.

When one is not free, one is not acting from the laws of one's own (rational) nature. In such cases one is thinking or acting on the basis of an external object, an object external to one's own (rational) nature. Spinoza conceives of the passions fundamentally along these lines, as external objects and as arising from outside us. He writes that:

34 THE STATE OF NATURE AND THE ORIGINS OF CIVIL SOCIETY

> Man's lack of power to moderate and restrain the affects I call bondage. For the man who is subject to affects is under the control, not of himself, but of fortune, in whose power he so greatly is that often, though he sees the better for himself, he is still forced to follow the worse.
>
> *(E4* pref.)

Passions arise from external causes. These affects arise because of a lack of power or impotence. As a result of our incapacity to control or moderate the affects, we are controlled by them. External objects, objects outside our rational domain, assail us and we are affected by sadness, joy, anger, etc. "Sadness," Spinoza writes, "is a man's passage from a greater to a lesser perfection" (*E3*, Definitions of the Affects, III). Sadness comes about because one's own nature is not determining one's activity. One's natural activity is stultified by being hijacked by an external source. This interruption results in a diminution of the perfection of the activity, a felt lessening of the optimal state. Feeling that lessening is pain or sadness. By contrast, if one were not assailed by external forces, one would not know the pain of sadness because all activities would be determined by one's own optimally active, self-governing nature.

It is impossible for a human being to live without being on the receiving end of external causes (*E4p4*). As it is with sadness, so it is with its counterpart, joy. Joy or pleasure occurs when an external object affects the body by increasing the activity of some part of it (although see *E3p59* where Spinoza claims that it is possible to experience joy arising from one's own healthful activity). When, for example, I eat too much chocolate cake I feel pleasure because the cake stimulates my tongue in such a way as to increase its perfection or health. Nevertheless, I later get a stomach ache because this same cake has a very different effect on my stomach. Both the experience of pleasure in my mouth and the experience of pain in my stomach, however, are affects or passions caused by an external object.

We are always affected by passions. It is impossible to do away with them (*E5* pref.). A human being is an organism constantly struggling against external forces that produce experiences of pleasure, pain, and all of the other affects. A human being can,

THE STATE OF NATURE AND THE ORIGINS OF CIVIL SOCIETY 35

therefore, never be entirely free. Freedom is always a matter of degree. Spinoza writes in the *Political Treatise* that "it is not in every man's power always to use reason and to be at the highest pitch of human freedom, but yet he always endeavors as far as in him lies to preserve his own being" (*PT* 2.8). Within every human being there is a constant battle between the activity of one's own nature (reason) and the external forces that are constantly imposing themselves. One can never achieve perfect rationality or freedom and so invulnerability to the affects, but one's activity can be more or less rational and directive, and so more or less free.

THE STATE OF NATURE

There are many competing conceptions of the state of nature in the philosophical literature. Some argue that it is (or was) a state of peace and equality (Rousseau). More commonly it is argued (by Hobbes, for example) that the state of nature is to be imagined as a situation dominated by strife, violence, and fear. In whatever way the state of nature is imagined and described, there is general agreement on one point, namely, the state of nature is a state of freedom. As we have seen, it is this freedom that is generative of a contract designed to offset the insecurity attending the state of nature.

Spinoza separates himself from this understanding of the state of nature as a state of freedom by arguing that the state of nature is actually one of *bondage*. The source of this bondage is the fear and anxiety that all must experience in a state of nature. One is constantly under threat of violence. Spinoza writes in the *Theological-Political Treatise* that "there is no one who does not live pervaded with anxiety whilst living surrounded by hostility, hatred, anger and deceit and who does not strive to avoid these insofar as they can" (*TTP* 16.5). In the *Ethics* Spinoza defines fear as "an inconstant sadness, born of the idea of a future or past thing whose outcome we to some extent doubt" (*E*3, Definitions of the Affects, XIII exp.). Because fear is a kind of sadness, one which waxes and wanes due to circumstance, it is a diminution of our perfection and virtue. The state of nature renders one less free because we are vulnerable to anxiety and fear. In this way Spinoza differs importantly from

36 THE STATE OF NATURE AND THE ORIGINS OF CIVIL SOCIETY

Hobbes. Both agree that there will be great anxiety in a state of nature, but only Spinoza believes that this anxiety diminishes freedom.

For Spinoza, the problems in a state of nature only get worse over time. He writes that: "insofar as men are torn by affects which are passions, they can be contrary to one another" (*E*4p34). The more subject to the passions we are, the more we disagree with one another and act contrary to each other's (and to our own) interests. Spinoza explains in the *Ethics* that "because [men] are subject to the affects (by *E*4p4c), which far surpass man's power, or virtue (by *E*4p6), they are often drawn in different directions (by *E*4p33) and are contrary to one another (by *E*4p34)" (*E*4p37s2). The affects (especially anxiety and fear) created by the state of nature generate rivalry and conflict. This conflict increases the fear, which in turn causes more conflict, which in turn causes more fear, and so on. Spinoza's psychology, therefore, predicts that a state of nature is necessarily one of continually escalating fear and conflict, and so, escalating bondage and slavery.

While Spinoza conceives of the state of nature to be one of bondage and conflict, he also considers it one free of claims of justice or injustice. Spinoza writes:

> In the state of nature there is no one who by common consent is Master of anything, nor is there anything in Nature which can be said to be this man's and not that man's. Instead all things belong to all. So in the state of nature, there cannot be conceived any will to give to each his own, or to take away from someone what is his. That is, in the state of nature nothing is done which can be called just or unjust.
> (*E*4p37s2)

Contra Locke, there is no ownership or private property in the state of nature. At best there is, as Rousseau says, mere possession (*Social Contract* 1.8). This absence of justice would seem *prima facie* to constitute a considerable freedom. As our actions in a state of nature are not constrained by justice, we might wonder if the state of nature doesn't in fact allow its inhabitants to be *freer* in some important respects. But the kind of "freedom" enjoyed here is not the kind of freedom that Spinoza is interested in. Along

THE STATE OF NATURE AND THE ORIGINS OF CIVIL SOCIETY   37

with classical republican authors, such as Rousseau and Montesquieu, and, surprisingly, the "liberal" Locke in some passages in the *Second Treatise on Government* (e.g. 6.63), Spinoza accepts the idea that freedom is *not* increased by the absence of law. Freedom in Spinoza is not Hobbes' "silence of the law". Freedom is not increased by anarchy. Rather, according to the classical republicans, freedom is freedom from arbitrary interference, and "arbitrary" here means "not governed by public rules". Republican freedom (from *arbitrary* interference) is very different from negative freedom (from *any* interference). Of necessity any law limits negative freedom, but certain laws can dramatically increase (positive) republican freedom (if they limit arbitrary interference). Spinoza's conception of freedom as acting only in accordance with those laws that derive from your own nature is an analogue to republican freedom – both enhance autonomy. His conception of freedom has more in common with Machiavelli, Rousseau, and even Locke in some passages, than with Hobbes' simple negative liberty. When one is free, according to Spinoza, one is following reason and living in accordance with laws. It follows that anarchy of any sort results in bondage and slavery. When free, according to Spinoza, one is following those laws that follow from one's (true) nature, the laws of reason. The lack of a sovereign and of established legal institutions is therefore a great hindrance to human freedom precisely because the anarchic conflict that results from the different passions causes interference with one's own ability to follow the laws of one's own nature. The reason why we cannot be free in a state of nature is that this state is not in accord with the laws of human nature.

THE NEED FOR CIVIL SOCIETY

Given Spinoza's views on human psychology and freedom, it is clear what must be done to quit the bondage of the state of nature. We need to make it possible to live according to rational laws that will have the effect of reducing the unpredictability (arbitrariness) and fear that is endemic to the state of nature. We need common laws to which we all subscribe and which will regulate our interactions. These laws, however, are not to be grounded on the affects or individual desire, but instead on reason. Spinoza writes that:

38 THE STATE OF NATURE AND THE ORIGINS OF CIVIL SOCIETY

> If we also reflect that without mutual help, and the cultivation of reason, human beings necessarily live in great misery ... we shall realize very clearly that it was necessary for people to combine together in order to live in security and prosperity ... They would, however, have had no hope of achieving this had they confined themselves only to the promptings of desire – for, by the laws of appetite, everyone is drawn in different directions. Thus, they had to make a firm decision, and reach agreement, to decide everything by the sole dictate of reason.
>
> (*TTP* 16.5)

The laws that are to govern us must be rational for three distinct reasons. First, "only insofar as men live according to the guidance of reason, must they always agree in nature" (*E*4p35). The only way that we will be able to find common ground and agreement among ourselves is to live in accordance with what we all have in common – reason.

Second, such laws of reason are in accord with human nature and so by following them we become free. Spinoza writes that "the freest state ... is that whose laws are founded on sound reason; for there each man can be free whenever he wishes, that is, he can live under the guidance of reason with his whole mind" (*TTP* 16.10; see also *PT* 3.7). In a state where the laws are the dictates of reason, and as we shall see this is a state that has reduced the power of the religious authorities, one becomes free by obeying the laws. In the *Ethics* Spinoza writes that: "a man who is guided by reason is more free in a state, where he lives according to a common decision, than in solitude, where he obeys only himself" (*E*4p73). One who is guided by reason prefers to live by the general decision of a community because, Spinoza thinks, this common decision (a kind of "general will") is less likely to be driven by arbitrary passion. Spinoza writes that: "it is almost impossible that the majority of a large assembly would agree on the same irrational decision" (*TTP* 16.9). Given that passions are arbitrary and random, they are likely to be randomly distributed throughout the community. Thus, in any large assembly the different passions will tend to cancel each other out and the general decision is more likely to be rational. This general decision-making presumption (which is remarkably similar to Madison's in

THE STATE OF NATURE AND THE ORIGINS OF CIVIL SOCIETY 39

Federalist 51) also obtains on an individual level. So long as the solitary individual follows his own lights, and is thereby alienated from the community, he is more liable to error and miscalculation than when he follows the general decision of the whole community. In the *Political Treatise* Spinoza argues that: "nobody acts in a way contrary to what his own reason prescribes in so far as he does that which the laws of the commonwealth require to be done" (*PT* 3.6). And in the *Theological-Political Treatise*, Spinoza memorably writes:

> It is not, I contend, the purpose of the state to turn people from rational beings into beasts or automata, but rather to allow their minds and bodies to develop in their own ways in security and enjoy the free use of reason, and not to participate in conflicts based on hatred, anger or deceit or in malicious disputes with each other. Therefore, the true purpose of the state is in fact freedom.
>
> (*TTP* 20.6)

Following the laws of the State does not enslave one, but rather frees one from passions and anxieties that keep one in bondage.

Third and finally, the laws of reason "aim at nothing but men's true interest" (*TTP* 16.5). Insofar as we are rational we are acting in the best interests of humanity. "The greatest good of those who seek virtue [to live rationally] is common to all, and can be enjoyed by all equally" (*E*4p36). *Prima facie* it seems as though reason would sometimes lead to disagreement. Consider a case of limited resources, where there is only a limited amount of food over which two people are competing. In this case each individual will reason that it is in his own best interest to take all the food for himself. Thus, it would appear that, contrary to what Spinoza suggests, conflicts arise precisely because of competing self-regarding calculations. But for Spinoza, this objection is misguided, and not a counter-example to the claim that rationality always harmonizes. For Spinoza, the aforementioned conflict does not arise on account of a shared rationality, but from the fact that each prefers himself to the

40 THE STATE OF NATURE AND THE ORIGINS OF CIVIL SOCIETY

other. It is their *difference* that causes the conflict, not their similarity.

For Spinoza, the more we follow reason, the more we act not only in our own individual best interest, but in the best interest of all other human beings. Spinoza explains this point at some length in the *Ethics*, where he argues first that deception is against the laws of reason and is unjustifiable. He then deals with a fairly obvious objection: "What if a man could save himself from the present danger of death by treachery? Would not the principle of preserving his own being recommend, without qualification, that he be treacherous?" (*E*4p72s). Spinoza's answer is clear:

> The reply to this is the same. If reason should recommend that, it would recommend it to all men. And so reason would recommend, without qualification, that men make agreements, join forces, and have common rights only by deception – i.e., that really they have no common rights. This is absurd.

> (*E*4p72s)

Reason will never prompt an agent to act in such a way that her (self-)interest stands in conflict with her fellow human beings' interest. If the agent is acting solely from the dictates of reason, then necessarily these dictates are equally in the best interest of all human beings.

To quit the state of nature a powerful force needs to be established that will impose rational laws on the community. Such laws of reason must be transformed into enforceable laws because (i) they are the only laws that will be widely agreed upon; (ii) they are the laws that make freedom possible; and (iii) they aim at the general good. How are the laws of reason to be transformed into the general laws of the community, for not everyone obeys reason? Most people are governed by the passions. The political challenge is to find a means to combat the passions that cause irrational behavior and opinions contrary to the laws of reason. In general, Spinoza believes that the only counterbalance to a certain affect is an opposite affect of at least equal strength (*E*4p7). Thus, the State needs to create a contrary affect (a counter force) of equal power to offset that which is causing the various irrationalities

THE STATE OF NATURE AND THE ORIGINS OF CIVIL SOCIETY 41

that disrupt potential political life. That affect is fear. Spinoza writes that:

> The main difference between [the state of nature and civil society] is this, that in the civil order all men fear the same things, and all men have the same grounds of security, the same way of life. But this does not deprive the individual of his faculty of judgment, for he who has resolved to obey all the commands of the commonwealth, whether through fear of its power or love of tranquility, is surely providing for his own security and his own advantage in his own way.

> *(PT* 3.3)

The sovereign must create rational laws and then back them up with a credible threat of punishment for those who disobey. This credible threat of punishment will create fear that will act as a counter to those passions that may cause one to act contrary to reason and the laws of the State. This obedience through fear, strong enough to combat the desire to follow the affects, is however just the first stage in this civilizing process. Over time and through the guidance of reason, fear is attenuated and gives itself over to a reasoned awareness of the benefit of living in common with others. At this point obedience to the law is not grounded in fear but in reason. "A man who is guided by reason," Spinoza writes, "is not led to obey by fear ... [but] insofar as he strives to live freely, desires to maintain the principle of common life and common advantage" (*E*4p73d). Similarly, Spinoza argues that the more rational one becomes, the more one will act rightly. He writes:

> For if everyone were readily led by the guidance of reason alone and recognized the supreme advantage and necessity of the state, everyone would utterly detest deceit and stand fully by their promises with the utmost fidelity because of their concern for this highest good of preserving the state ...

> *(TTP* 16.7)

In becoming more rational one obeys the laws because of an understanding that in doing so one strengthens the state and *thereby* makes oneself and all of one's fellow citizens more free.

42 THE STATE OF NATURE AND THE ORIGINS OF CIVIL SOCIETY

Living in the State, safe under secure and reasonable laws, is, therefore, the highest good. It makes freedom possible, not to do whatever you wish, but rather to have the opportunity to be all that you can be.

But what about those laws, and those sovereigns that are utterly unreasonable? States often promulgate laws that are not beneficial and quite irrational. Should these laws be obeyed? Spinoza says that they should. He writes that:

> It follows that unless we wish to be enemies of government and to act against reason, which urges us to defend the government with all our strength, we are obliged to carry out absolutely all the commands of the sovereign power, however absurd they may be. Reason too bids us to do so; it is a choice of the lesser of two evils.
>
> (*TTP* 16.8)

If the State passes bad laws, they ought nevertheless to be followed because not following them weakens the State and so weakens the conditions necessary for one's own freedom. Perhaps this is justifiable because, at least within certain political arrangements, there exists the chance for a reconsideration of those bad laws. In any event, Spinoza is not suggesting that whatever the State promulgates is *ipso facto* good and beneficial. As we have seen, Spinoza rejects the claim that might makes right, and he has a keen sense of human frailty. Both individual citizens and the sovereign (assembly) are in fact sometimes led astray by the affects. (Only God, the one infinite substance, is entirely free from passive affects.) The healthier the State, however, the more rational the laws will be, and the more they will tend to enhance the human good.

FORMING A CIVIL SOCIETY

A contentious question in the literature on Spinoza's political philosophy that arises from the foregoing is this: How is civil society created? We suggest that one cannot separate the "how" from the "why" civil society is created. We have already seen that, for Spinoza, unlike Hobbes, civil society is created to enhance freedom not curb it. The sovereign is more than a nightwatchman, or ought to

THE STATE OF NATURE AND THE ORIGINS OF CIVIL SOCIETY 43

be, for he is charged with maximizing human potential, not just keeping the peace. Spinoza writes:

> Human society can thus be formed without any alienation of natural right, and the contract can be preserved in its entirety with complete fidelity, only if every person transfers all the power they possess to society, and society alone retains the supreme natural right over all things, i.e., supreme power, which all must obey, either of their own free will or through fear of the ultimate punishment.

(*TTP* 16.8)

The Rousseau-like quality of this message should not go unnoticed, and later in this book we will suggest connections between Spinoza and Rousseau. For the moment, however, consider why a contract is even necessary if there is no alienation (relinquishing) of any natural right or freedom. Consider a group held in slavery, or somehow enslaved by their own lack of power. These unfortunates have no freedom whatsoever, or at least very little freedom. If such are freed, or educated out of their self-induced ignorance, have we violated any natural rights? We have not. Freeing one from slavery does not limit natural rights, for one possesses neither rights nor power in a state of bondage. So, it seems we can free slaves without asking for their consent. Since, according to Spinoza, as we are all enslaved to our passions in the state of nature – and note that for Spinoza it is impossible that we ever finally rid ourselves of these passions – freeing us from this state does not require our consent. While Spinoza speaks of a "contract" and the "transfer of power", his language is loose and needs to be read in the context of his revisionist notions of freedom, power, and right.

So does Spinoza offer a social contract theory? No, if we think of a social contract like that of Hobbes or Locke. Spinoza's theory of political legitimacy is genuinely original. While using the languageof the classical social contract theorists, he is engaged in a project that does not take the *justification* of political authority as paramount. Under the rubric of *weak normativity*, we have been suggesting that, for Spinoza, political authority is not grounded in consent that generates an obligation, but rather is grounded in a felt need that the sovereign authority has the power, and hence the

THE STATE OF NATURE AND THE ORIGINS OF CIVIL SOCIETY

right, to make us free and better able to lead active lives. We *should* obey the sovereign in all things in exactly this "weakly normative" sense. There is no robust moral obligation to do so, but it certainly is to our benefit because it is in our own best interest. Insofar as we are rational, we recognize this. Only in that sense do we "consent".

CONCLUSION

In this chapter we have examined Spinoza's views on the state of nature and the social contract. We have argued that contrary to classical social contract theorists, Spinoza argues that the state of nature is a state of bondage, not of freedom. Freedom is possible only when the laws of reason, generally in the form of civic statutes, are imposed on a community and backed up with a credible threat of punishment for those who do not obey. The laws should be based on reason because (i) they are the only laws that can command a majority acceptance, (ii) obeying them is conducive to freedom, and finally (iii) they aim at what is in the best interest of all. When Spinoza says that citizens of a state have agreed or consented to obey these laws, he is saying nothing more than that they realize it is in their own best interest to obey.

FURTHER READING

For studies on Spinoza's anti-Hobbesian conception of freedom and the role that this understanding of freedom plays in his overall philosophy, see Kisner (2011) and Adkins (2009), as well as J. Steinberg (2008, 2009) and Nadler (2005). D. Garrett (1990 and 2010) places Spinoza in conversation with Hobbes on the beginnings of civil society, and Rosenthal (1998) elucidates the nature of the collective action there involved.

4

CRITIQUE OF TRADITIONAL BIBLICAL RELIGION

INTRODUCTION

In this chapter and the next we turn to Spinoza's influential discussion of religion in the *Theological-Political Treatise*. Many of Spinoza's most influential and important *political* arguments concern the nature and purpose of religion in the state. Given the time and place in which he wrote, outlined in our first chapter, this is perhaps not surprising. It is hard to overstate the effect that Spinoza's discussion had on his contemporaries. This section of the *TTP* was by far the most widely read and discussed – and the most controversial. After its (anonymous) publication in 1670, the book was almost immediately banned in every European land on account of what is written in these chapters (Israel 2001: chapter 36). These chapters shocked even radicals like Hobbes. When Hobbes read the book he disapproved and said that even "I durst not write so boldly" (Curley 1992). The *TTP* was called a book "forged in hell" (which is also the title of Nadler's 2011 study of Spinoza's political

46 CRITIQUE OF TRADITIONAL BIBLICAL RELIGION

and religious views). Whereas Hobbes' public views on traditional biblical religion are ambiguous, muddled, and confusing, Spinoza's views are clear and unambiguous. Spinoza rejected traditional biblical religion in *all* of its monotheistic forms, and argued that its influence in political life should be significantly curtailed. The subordination of religious authority to civil authority constitutes a critical component of Spinoza's political philosophy. Unsurprisingly, his arguments were seen as a direct threat to the Christendom Model of society.

To reject as false *all* traditional biblical religion was a shocking and daring position in the seventeenth century. Before Spinoza only a few cranks and oddballs had dared to do so. Although the *TTP* was published anonymously, it quickly became an open secret that Spinoza had written it. Spinoza was thus the first to bear the brunt of taking such a radical position. On the basis of its anti-religious claims the *TTP* became a defining book among "freethinkers" and radicals over the next few centuries. Despite being on the proscribed list in all European countries, the book found its way into almost every major European library during Spinoza's lifetime (Israel 2001: chapter 6). The *TTP* made Spinoza (in)famous. The attacks on the book came fast and furious. Spinoza, however, never publically replied to any of his critics – he was dead seven years after its publication. The notoriety he garnered after the publication of the *TTP* was such that it prevented him from publishing his monumental *Ethics* in the late 1670s. Spinoza was too much in the public eye to take another risk by publishing yet another "atheistic" tract.

In this chapter we examine in some detail Spinoza's critique of traditional biblical religion. Although Spinoza is critical of traditional religion, it is very important to clarify his *positive* account of the proper role of religion in political life, and we do so in the following chapters. We begin this chapter with an examination of the role that traditional biblical religion played in the Christendom Model of society. After this outline we then examine Spinoza's four central critiques of traditional biblical religion, critiques of (1) the nature of revelation (or prophecy), (2) the possibility of miracles, (3) the content of revelation or the divine law, and (4) the interpretation of Scripture.

CRITIQUE OF TRADITIONAL BIBLICAL RELIGION **47**

TRADITIONAL BIBLICAL RELIGION IN THE CHRISTENDOM MODEL

Traditional biblical religion as understood by Spinoza is based on four related foundational claims. These claims are essential to all forms of biblical religion and so to the Christendom Model concerning the relation of the Church to the State. Undermining these claims calls into doubt, therefore, not only traditional patterns of religious belief and behavior, but also the nature of all seventeenth-century political institutions as well. These critiques form the heart of the destructive and revisionist project of Spinoza's *Theological-Political Treatise*. After these four critiques have undermined existing political theory, Spinoza can then offer his alternative conception of political society. The four foundational claims are:

(1) *Prophecy*: God spoke to human beings by means of prophets and provided them with certain propositional information (revelations) about himself and about how best to live.
(2) *Miracles*: Prophecy is validated in part by the prophet's ability to perform miracles. Miracles are understood as violations of the laws of nature. The ability to perform miracles proves that the prophet is close to God, favored by God, and so his teachings (revelations) can be trusted.
(3) *Divine Law*: The most important part of God's revelations to human beings by means of prophets concerns the divine law. This law concerns a way of life that brings human beings closer to God. As finite beings, we could not have discovered the divine law on our own and so we need a beneficent God to reveal it to us.
(4) *The Scriptures*: The true intention and trajectory of the divine law may be found by interpreting the Scriptures. These Scriptures are the Word of God and so they are infallible when interpreted correctly.

There is much debate about how to understand these four foundational claims within and among the different religious traditions. Catholics and Protestants have important disagreements concerning, for example, the interpretation of Scripture. Nevertheless, these

48 CRITIQUE OF TRADITIONAL BIBLICAL RELIGION

claims were not controversial in the early modern period. They were part of the "common sense" of the period. They were so ubiquitously believed that they went almost entirely unchallenged. The debates before Spinoza were primarily confessional in nature. The question was how to understand these claims. Spinoza was revolutionary in challenging not one confession or another, but in challenging the foundations of biblical religion itself – and with it an entire conception of society and politics.

CRITIQUE ONE: ON PROPHECY (OR REVELATION)

Spinoza begins his radical critique by challenging the first fundamental claim of biblical religion, namely, that God spoke to human beings by means of prophets and provided them with certain propositional information about himself and how best to live. Spinoza's general approach to revelation is to *naturalize* it. By this we mean that Spinoza "universalizes" the phenomenon so that it ceases to possess a unique epistemological status. In fact, this naturalizing or universalizing tendency is the general theme of the four critiques.

Part of what makes Spinoza's critique of prophecy so intriguing is that he, perhaps surprisingly, couches it in pious language. A casual reader might mistake Spinoza for a somewhat odd, but rather traditional, theist. Only rarely does he claim outright that some cherished view of traditional theism is false. More often he argues that he is merely attempting to "interpret" or "understand" traditional religious claims. Spinoza's penchant for using religious discourse while arguing against religion has puzzled many. The key to understanding Spinoza's approach can be found in the *Treatise on the Emendation of the Intellect.* Here Spinoza discusses his method of using ordinary discourse in revisionist ways. In a revealing remark he writes,

> We are forced, before we do anything else, to assume certain rules of living as good. Firstly, to speak according to the power of understanding of ordinary people, and to do whatever does not interfere with our attaining our purpose. For we can gain a considerable advantage, if we yield as much to their understanding as we can. In this way, they will give a favorable hearing to the truth.
>
> (*TIE* 17)

CRITIQUE OF TRADITIONAL BIBLICAL RELIGION **49**

If Spinoza had explicitly claimed that the Bible is not divinely inspired, that the prophets are not wise and suffer from over-active imaginations, and that there is no personal God, his works would never have received a hearing. The only way for Spinoza to gain a hearing and to be taken seriously was to present his views in a rhetorically effective manner, in such a way as not to offend the pious sensibilities of his contemporaries. By using the language of the ordinary reader, and even those who are "moderately enlightened", Spinoza will be able to convince them to hear him out. He will be able to carry the reader along, as we might say. At first the reader may take Spinoza to be explicating religious doctrine, then on the basis of this shared project the reader may be led to consider new interpretations, and only over time and as a result of effort and a desire to follow the argument wherever it leads, the reader will sense the full scale of Spinoza's unorthodoxy. (Remember that Spinoza was expelled and ostracized from the Jewish community in Amsterdam for heresy in 1656.) We believe that this is Spinoza's way of proceeding in the *TTP* and why he adopts the language of his opponents. Reflecting on Spinoza's words, as he wished, leads the reader from perhaps a liberal Protestantism through successive stages and ultimately to Spinozistic atheism. We should note, however, that few readers have actually followed this path in the way that Spinoza intended. In this sense Spinoza's rhetoric fooled nobody. His intentions became clear immediately.

Let us see Spinoza at work in the way he intends. In explicating the biblical notion of prophecy, of supernatural knowledge and divine intercession in human affairs, Spinoza writes that:

> Here at the outset we must note that the Jews never specify intermediate or particular causes and take no notice of them, but owing to religion or piety, or (in the common phrase) "for devotion's sake", refer everything back to God. For example, if they have made some money by a business transaction, they say that it has been given to them by God; if they happen to want something, they say God has stirred their heart ... Therefore we should not consider as prophecy or supernatural knowledge everything that Scripture claims God says to someone but only what Scripture expressly designates as prophecy or revelation ...
>
> (*TTP* 1.6)

50 CRITIQUE OF TRADITIONAL BIBLICAL RELIGION

In this passage Spinoza notes that due to religious piety, and for no other reason, the Jews refer everything to God. God is invoked as the author of all acts and events, outcomes, and hopes. No other source or "intermediate" cause is mentioned, due to a pious deference to God. An uncritical interpretation of mundane events would be to see God's hand in everything. Spinoza rejects such an interpretation. Mundane affairs have mundane causes, and much that passes for "prophecy" (a divine intercession in human affairs) can likewise be explained by means of natural causes. Spinoza's account here is deflationary, but, importantly, it is not outright dismissive and is grounded in critical analyses of biblical texts and traditional understandings. Given the radical nature of his views, in this case the naturalizing of prophecy, his mode of presentation is cautious and sensible.

Spinoza hides his revisionist metaphysics within his biblical hermeneutics in the *TTP*. This radical metaphysics appears explicitly in the *Ethics* (which he commenced writing before he began writing the *TTP*), but at the time the *Ethics* was published Spinoza was no longer alive, so he was not called on to defend his views in person. In the *TTP* only glimpses of it can be seen, and his argumentation there does not presuppose the full-blown monism expounded in the *Ethics*. The (deflationary) naturalism of his biblical critique in the *TTP* is grounded in his own biblical hermeneutics, as we have just seen in the example above. The Bible itself, correctly understood, is consistent with Spinozistic naturalism. Spinoza's biblical critique is an "internalist" one, and he is interpreting the text from itself (*sola Scriptura*). He is not coming to the text from the "outside" and finding it wanting. It is not the case that the "New Philosophy" gives the lie to the Bible. Spinoza repeatedly claims that faith and philosophy do not conflict, rather "each has its own kingdom" (*TTP* 15.9), and indeed "the principal purpose of the whole work" is "to separate faith from philosophy" (*TTP* 14.2). So, it is on the basis of precise textual analyses that Spinoza defends the radical conclusions he reaches about the nature of prophecy, of miracles, and of divine law as the intentions of the biblical authors, properly understood. By contrast, institutional religion and its support for a variety of supernaturalist readings of the Bible has gotten it wrong because it has interpreted the text in such a way as to support its own self-serving agenda. Spinoza sees himself as a dispassionate

CRITIQUE OF TRADITIONAL BIBLICAL RELIGION   51

reader of the text and also as a reformer, like a Protestant reformer intent on prying the truth from the text – but his conclusions are of course far more radical.

We now turn to an examination of Spinoza's arguments concerning the nature of prophecy. Spinoza begins his critique of the first fundamental claim of traditional biblical religion with some definitions. He writes that:

> Prophecy or revelation is certain knowledge about something revealed to men by God. A prophet is someone who interprets things revealed by God to those who cannot themselves achieve certain knowledge of them and can therefore only grasp by simple faith what has been revealed.
>
> (*TTP* 1.1)

There are interesting things to note in the definition. First, a prophet is not the voice or mere mouthpiece of God. Instead the prophet "interprets the things revealed by God to those who cannot themselves achieve certain knowledge of them." The role of the prophet on Spinoza's view is quintessentially political, a legacy from Plato, al-Farabi, and Maimonides. The prophet helps those who cannot help themselves to understand. Prophetic wisdom is moral and political. He teaches moral truths to simple people. The prophet does not reveal new knowledge unobtainable by human reason and empirical inquiry. Spinoza clearly wishes to counter a supernaturalist view of prophecy. Nevertheless, the truths the prophet teaches are divine, dependent on knowledge of God. Indeed, for Spinoza, all that we know by the natural light of reason is "divine" in this sense. Scientists are no different from prophets in this regard – both ground their claims in the natural light of reason, even as the mode of discovery and the presentations of their respective truths to their respective audiences differ. Spinoza writes that:

> What we know by the natural light of reason depends on knowledge of God and his eternal decrees alone ... Natural knowledge has as much right to be called divine as any other kind of knowledge, since it is the nature of God, so far as we share in it, and God's decrees, that may be said to dictate to us.
>
> (*TTP* 1.2)

52 CRITIQUE OF TRADITIONAL BIBLICAL RELIGION

The traditional distinction between revealed (prophetic) truths that are outside the scope of human reason and the truths of natural theology and science that are attained through unaided reason is rejected by Spinoza. There are no truths that are in principle "above human reason". This claim is a startling one because many different aspects of the universe do seem to be beyond our capacities of comprehension. Spinoza believes that we, on account of our finite minds, cannot fully comprehend the "order and connection" of causes in nature. But we can know, he thinks, the basic truths and laws that govern nature. We can predict in individual cases how things will move in accordance with the laws of nature. We are limited only insofar as we can only do a limited number of these calculations at any one time. Our understanding of nature on Spinoza's view is a lot like our understanding of mathematics. We can understand all of the truths of inference and the basic mathematical entities (numbers, lines, planes, etc.). We are limited only insofar as we cannot actually do every deduction that can in principle be performed.

Given Spinoza's extremely optimistic view of human knowledge, he makes an inference that removes any epistemological uniqueness that the prophet might possess. He writes that:

> Since therefore our minds possess the power to form such notions from this alone – that it objectively contains within itself the nature of God and participates in it – and explain the nature of things and teach us how to live, we may rightly affirm that it is the nature of the mind, in so far as it is thus conceived, that is the primary source of divine revelation.

(*TTP* 1.4)

For Spinoza, then, revelations come not directly from God, but from the *idea* of God in the mind of the prophet. Furthermore, the idea of God is common to all people everywhere. Prophets are not, therefore, special individuals set apart by God for some important mission and message. Rather they are ordinary individuals who inferred from their idea of God certain truths about how to live. Anyone sufficiently rational in this way could likewise infer these truths from her own innate idea of God.

CRITIQUE OF TRADITIONAL BIBLICAL RELIGION 53

While prophets are not essentially different from other human beings, there is something they share in common with one another, namely, a robust imaginative faculty: "Everything that God revealed to the prophets was revealed to them either in words or in images, or by both these means together" (*TTP* 1.7). By contrast to all the other prophets, Spinoza distinguishes Moses and Mosaic prophecy by noting that: "it was with a real voice that God revealed to Moses the Laws which he wished to be given to the Hebrews" (*TTP* 1.8). This, in Spinoza's view, is exactly what distinguishes Moses from the other prophets. The Mosaic prophecy took place without any appeal to images. The other prophets did not hear a *real* voice (*TTP* 1.17). To understand exactly this distinction between Mosaic prophecy and all other prophecy one must take into account Spinoza's distinction between the intellect and the imagination.

According to Spinoza, the imagination is the ability of the mind to form *images*. The imagination is contrasted with the intellect, which latter concerns *understandings*. The distinction is a traditional one, and can be found as early as Plato. The important point to note is that images are, according to Spinoza, always fragmentary and inadequate. To imagine something is not to know and understand it in an abiding and unassailable (scientific) way, which roots understanding in causes. Only when one understands something in a causally grounded way that takes place without any images, does one know it as it really is. Understandings are in this way adequate or complete; images can never be, given their ephemeral and fragmentary nature (*E*2p28d). Thus, in claiming that "everything that God revealed to the prophets was revealed to them either in words or in images, or by both these means together" (*TTP* 1.7), Spinoza is deflating the pretensions of prophecy and the traditional understanding of it as a special form of divine insight and wisdom. Prophetic moral wisdom, grounded in the imaginative faculty, is true, and the perfect vehicle for instructing the mass of humankind in moral truth, as they will be motivated by images of an angry and loving God. Spinoza's view of the power of prophecy here owes much to medieval forebears such as Maimonides, though it should be noted that Maimonides understood the prophet as an analogue to the Platonic philosopher-king and

54 CRITIQUE OF TRADITIONAL BIBLICAL RELIGION

prophecy as a species of philosophical understanding, in sharp contrast to Spinoza.

It is important to underscore this distinction that Spinoza makes between the prophets and the philosophers. He writes that:

> The prophets were not endowed with more perfect minds than others but only a more vivid power of imagination, as the scriptural narratives also abundantly show ... [But] those who are most powerful in imagination are less good at merely understanding things; those who have trained and powerful intellects have a more modest power of imagination and have it under better control, reining it in, so to speak, and not confusing it with understanding.
>
> *(TTP* 2.1)

For Spinoza, prophecy is fraught with a certain danger, given its imaginative grounding. The problem is that images are always fragmentary and so cannot capture the nature or essence of a thing. Spinoza concludes that:

> Plain imagination does not of its own nature provide certainty, as every clear and distinct idea [that is, idea of the intellect] does. In order that we may be certain of what we imagine, imagination must necessarily be assisted by something, and that something is reason. It follows from this that prophecy by itself cannot provide certainty.
>
> *(TTP* 2.3)

The inadequacy of the prophet's imaginings is problematic even for the prophet himself. The imaginings must be accompanied by something else to guarantee their veracity. That is why

> Prophets always received a sign assuring them of what they had prophetically imagined ... in this respect, consequently, prophecy is inferior to natural knowledge since [the latter] has no need of any sign but provides certainty by its very nature. For this prophetic certainty was not mathematical certainty but only moral certainty.
>
> *(TTP* 2.3)

CRITIQUE OF TRADITIONAL BIBLICAL RELIGION 55

A prophet receives signs along with his revelations and these signs verify the moral truths. They take the place of the certainty and self-evidential nature that the scientist or mathematician has regarding her truths. But what is this "moral certainty" and how does it differ from mathematical certainty? A clue is found later in the same chapter, when Spinoza writes that:

> All prophetic certainty therefore was grounded upon three things:
>
> (1) that the matters revealed were very vividly imagined, as we are affected by objects when we are awake
> (2) that they were accompanied by a sign
> (3) most importantly, that the minds of the prophets were directed exclusively to what is right and good.
>
> (*TTP* 2.5)

The moral certainty that the prophet achieves, therefore, is only as much certainty as one could get from a vivid experience (that may not have been shared by others), which is accompanied by an unusual happening (a sign), and limited and conformable to a specific domain of life (the right and good.) This last, limiting condition is important for Spinoza, as he is determined to separate off prophecy, and its truth, from its traditional pretensions to metaphysics. As noted, the message of the prophets is moral and political, and it is offered for the moral betterment and political stability of the community. There is moral certainty, a verification procedure in the moral realm, and there is moral knowledge that the prophets have attained. But the true nature of prophecy and its accompanying verification procedure are not "scientific" in any sense.

Spinoza is clear that the "verifying" signs are indexed to the nature and constitution of each individual prophet: "Signs were given according to the prophet's beliefs and understanding" (*TTP* 2.6). This adaptation of prophecy to the beliefs of the individual prophet explains some of the contradictions in Scripture (*TTP* 2.18). Each particular prophet imagined things differently. Thus, in the revelations brought forth and taught by the prophets there is a mixture of (universal) moral truths and idiosyncratic opinions, the particular ways by which the truths are presented. These

56 CRITIQUE OF TRADITIONAL BIBLICAL RELIGION

individual opinions can be disregarded and are not part of the revelation proper. Those moral truths that can be confirmed on the basis of reason we know to have been correctly inferred by the prophet from the prophet's own idea of God by means of vivid images.

We have so far been focusing on Spinoza's view of prophecy as found in the Hebrew Bible. But Spinoza has interesting things to say about Jesus and his paradigmatic role as a moral teacher as well. In a famous passage, Spinoza writes that:

> I do not believe that anyone has reached such a degree of perfection above others except Christ, to whom the decrees of God which guide men to salvation were revealed not by words or visions but directly; and that is why God revealed himself to the Apostles through the mind of Christ, as he did, formerly, to Moses by means of a heavenly voice. Therefore the voice of Christ may be called the voice of God, like the voice which Moses heard ... Here I must point out that I am not speaking at all of the things that certain churches affirm of Christ nor do I deny them; for I freely admit that I do not understand them ... If Moses spoke with God face to face as a man with his friend (that is, through the mediation of two bodies), Christ communicated with God from mind to mind.

(*TTP* 1.18–19)

Spinoza considers Jesus as the greatest prophet, greater even than Moses, who heard God with a real voice, but not with the intellect unaided. Only Jesus's revelations came by means of the intellect alone. His moral message is truly universal, with no admixture of the imagination. The universality of his message is a function of its not being indexed to the nature and constitution of any particular human being. It is as though Jesus is a disembodied mind through which the moral truth is transmitted to humankind. Jesus's teachings are in no way contingently true. He had an understanding of the moral truth beyond all other prophets. Needless to say, these moral truths are not to be identified with the teachings of the Churches concerning the nature and redemptive work of Christ.

CRITIQUE OF TRADITIONAL BIBLICAL RELIGION 57

In sum, traditional biblical religion has a mistaken view of prophecy. Prophecy is not supernatural. The prophets are moral teachers, whose wisdom and teaching are grounded in the imagination, underwritten by signs and wonders, and conformable to reason. Prophecy is the perfect vehicle by which to teach moral truths to the common people. The universality of the moral message is applicable to non-philosopher and philosopher alike, but the latter can put aside the "imaginative" rhetoric in which the moral truths are stated. The prophetic tradition, therefore, has no inherent *authority* on Spinoza's view. There is nothing in this tradition that is not available to all rational individuals, even though the imaginative presentation of prophecy is understandable given the great differences in the intellectual capacities of humankind. Institutional religion and churches, thus, are not repositories of secret wisdom. Spinoza's naturalization of prophecy has the effect of eliminating any special status claimed by religious authorities. This has significant implications for the Christendom Model of society because it implies that political authorities no longer need a religious imprimatur.

CRITIQUE TWO: ON MIRACLES

The revelations interpreted by prophets are confirmed by what Spinoza calls "signs" or "miracles". Spinoza begins his discussion of miracles by saying that men "classify any phenomenon whose cause is unknown by the common people 'divine' or the work of God" (*TTP* 6.1). These people, Spinoza writes, "call unusual works of nature miracles or works of God and do not want to know the natural causes of things" (*TTP* 6.1). A miracle, presumed by the many to be a violation of the laws of nature, is, on Spinoza's definition, a natural phenomenon whose cause is (presently) unknown. Miracle is a *relational* concept on this usage. Some event is miraculous relative to some observers (e.g., the common people), but not to others (e.g., scientists). This use of the term "miracle" we term a *relative miracle* because the event is "miraculous" to one only if one does not know the ultimate causal explanation for the event. For example, the drug offered to me by a doctor when I am sick may be miraculous ("amazing") to me (because I do not know

58 CRITIQUE OF TRADITIONAL BIBLICAL RELIGION

how it works), but not miraculous to the doctor (because he understands the medicinal capacities of the drug). According to this account, as science proceeds and becomes more widely accepted, miracles tend to disappear.

A relative miracle is contrasted with what are often called *Humean miracles*. A Humean miracle is a violation of the laws of nature *tout court*. These miracles are *absolute* miracles because they are miraculous from everyone's point of view. In Section X of *An Enquiry Concerning Human Understanding*, Hume famously argued that it is never rational to believe that a (Humean) miracle has occurred on the basis of testimony. Such (absolute) miracles, violations of the laws of nature caused directly by a transcendent God, are what most people understand by "miracle". In explicating what goes for common wisdom on the topic, Spinoza writes that the common people

> suppose the existence of God is proven by nothing more clearly than from what they perceive as nature failing to follow its normal course. For this reason they suppose that all those who explain or attempt to explain phenomena and miracles by natural causes, are doing away with God or at least divine providence.
>
> (*TTP* 6.1)

The common people (non-scientists) suppose that God's existence is proven by means of (Humean) miracles because they imagine God to be a powerful force distinct from the power of the universe. Thus, the argument goes, to prove his existence to us he would need to perform some action in nature that we can attribute to nothing in nature. We will then be required to look *beyond* nature for an explanation of this strange phenomenon. This is how the argument from miracles to the existence of God generally goes. Spinoza writes:

> Hence, they [common people] imagine that there are two powers, distinct from each other, the power of God and the power of natural things, and that the latter is determined by God in some way or, as most men think in our day, created by him. But what they understand by these powers, and what they understand by God and nature, they

CRITIQUE OF TRADITIONAL BIBLICAL RELIGION 59

certainly do not know, except that they imagine the power of God to be like the authority of royal majesty, and the power of nature to be like a force and impetus.

(*TTP* 6.1)

This inadequate understanding of God in Spinoza's view leads the unwary to an inadequate understanding of nature too. By imagining God to be like a king who issues commands, one misunderstands radically the relationship between God and the world. For Spinoza, a true understanding of the relationship between God and the world leads directly to his controversial identity of God and nature in the *Ethics* (*E*4 pref.), of which here in the *TTP* we may discern only a hint. But in chapter six of the *Theological-Political Treatise* Spinoza criticizes the common views, which he believes are essential to all traditional biblical religions, and proposes instead that there are only relative miracles. He defends three related theses in his chapter concerning miracles. These are:

(1) *Metaphysical Thesis:* "That nothing happens contrary to nature, but nature maintains an eternal, fixed, and immutable order".
(2) *Epistemic Thesis:* "That from miracles we cannot know about either the essence or the existence or the providence of God, but rather that all three are much better grasped from the fixed and unchanging order of nature".
(3) *Scriptural Thesis:* "I will show from some examples in the Bible that by decrees, volitions and providence of God, Scripture itself means nothing other than the order of nature which necessarily follows from his eternal law".

(*TTP* 6.2)

In the rest of this section we examine in some detail the arguments that Spinoza gives for each of these theses, which together form the backbone of his argument against the possibility of miracles.

DEFENSE OF THE METAPHYSICAL THESIS

The first important thesis concerning miracles that Spinoza defends we term the *Metaphysical Thesis*. This is the claim "that nothing

60 CRITIQUE OF TRADITIONAL BIBLICAL RELIGION

happens contrary to nature, but nature maintains an eternal, fixed, and immutable order" (*TTP* 6.2). This claim is far more radical than Hume's skepticism about miracles. Whereas Hume argued that it is almost never rational to believe that a miracle, a genuine violation of nature, has occurred, Spinoza argues that it is impossible that a miracle could ever occur. The consequences of this view are momentous. Spinoza is arguing here that it is *logically impossible* for petitionary prayers to God to be answered, just as it is logically impossible for the (fixed) order of nature to be violated. Spinoza's argument for the Metaphysical Thesis takes place in three steps. It follows a pattern of argument seen elsewhere in Spinoza. Spinoza begins with *prima facie* pious assumptions and ends with an (impious) naturalistic conclusion. Spinoza begins his defense by claiming that:

> From the fact that God's understanding is not distinct from God's will, we showed that we are asserting the same thing when we say that God wills something as when we say that God understands it. Hence by the same necessity by which it follows from the divine nature and perfection that God understands some thing as it is, it also follows that God wills it as it is.
>
> (*TTP* 6.3)

The identity of God's will and God's intellect is a traditional theological belief, at least as old as Maimonides and Aquinas. Notice that Spinoza commences his argument with the traditional understanding of God as a power distinct from the universe. He is not presupposing his own idiosyncratic conception of God as presented in the *Ethics*, a view that identifies God and Nature. Spinoza grounds his naturalism and denial of the possibility of miracles from the assumptions of traditional biblical religion itself. The belief in the identity of God's will and intellect comes about from the claim that God is absolutely simple. God has no parts. If God has no parts, then God cannot have an intellect distinct from his will because then he would have at least two parts, or aspects. Thus, God's intellect must be identical with his will.

The consequences of identifying God's will and intellect are significant, for on this account it is impossible for God to think

CRITIQUE OF TRADITIONAL BIBLICAL RELIGION 61

or cognize something without at the same time willing it. God cannot be imagined to ponder different options and then choose the best one, because as soon as he cognizes it, he instantiates it. This claim will lead Spinoza eventually to his necessitarianism (the view that everything that happens is logically necessary), but in his argument on miracles Spinoza draws a less controversial conclusion from the identity of God's will and intellect, namely, that: "Since nothing is necessarily true except by divine decree alone, it most clearly follows that the universal laws of nature are simply God's decrees and follow from the necessity and perfection of the divine nature" (*TTP* 6.3). How this passage relates to the identity of the will and the intellect in God is not immediately obvious. The key claim here is that "nothing is necessarily true except by divine decree alone". Spinoza implies that this claim follows from the claim that God's will and intellect are identical. But how does this inference work? Spinoza infers this conclusion from the identity of God's will and intellect because there is nothing that could make God's beliefs true except God's own actions. For God, to cognize something or some state of affairs is to will it into being. The very truth and being of some state of affairs follows from God's cognitive assent or "by divine decree alone". This position, or something seemingly like it, may have been held in antiquity by Parmenides, an early monist, who straightforwardly asserted that "thinking and being are the same".

For Spinoza (*contra* Leibniz), there are in God's intellect no unrealized possibilities. Given the identity of the intellect and will in God, God could have done nothing else. The laws of nature must follow from the very nature of God, and they must follow necessarily. Given God's absolute perfection, he thinks only the most perfect thoughts and so does only the most perfect things. From these claims, Spinoza then makes the dangerous inference. He writes:

> If anything therefore were to happen in nature that contradicted its universal laws, it would also necessarily contradict the decree and understanding and nature of God. Or if anyone were to assert that God does anything contrary to the laws of nature, he would at the

62 CRITIQUE OF TRADITIONAL BIBLICAL RELIGION

> same time be compelled to assert that God acts contrary to his own nature, than which nothing is more absurd.
>
> (*TTP* 6.3)

Given that the laws of nature must follow from God's essence, it is impossible that anything should happen that is contrary to these laws. If something happened contrary to these laws, then either God would have changed his nature or essence, or, equally impossible, something more powerful than God would have acted in opposition to him. Thus, "nothing happens in nature that contradicts its universal laws; and nothing occurs which does not conform to those laws or follow from them" (*TTP* 6.4). It is very important to note here that Spinoza's "traditional" argument against the possibility of miracles commences with generally accepted assumptions about the nature of divinity and divine power and ends with radical naturalism. The rhetorical strategy here employed seems quite sensible for one wishing to get a hearing for (what turn out to be) radically anti-religious views. Later in the *Ethics*, God is identified with Nature in a much more straightforward way.

Here is a short formalized version of this proof against the possibility of miracles:

(1) God wills the universal laws of nature. (Premise 1)
(2) God's will does not change. (Premise 2)
(3) Nothing is more powerful than God. (Premise 3)
(4) Imagine, *per impossibile*, that something occurred that violated the laws of nature. (Premise 4, for *reductio*)
(5) Then either (a) God did not will the laws of nature, (b) God's nature changed, or (c) something more powerful than God exists. (From 1–4)
(6) But (a) is ruled out by (1), (b) is ruled out by (2), and (c) is ruled out by (3). None of (a)–(c) could occur.
(7) Thus, Premise 4 is false. Nothing could occur that violates the laws of nature.

Spinoza believes that he has proven that no miracle could occur. Everything that happens must be in accord with the (unique) set of natural laws willed by God. As noted, the proof here is grounded in a traditional notion of the divine, but even in the later *Ethics* Spinoza will endorse a version of this argument even as he employs his own distinctive conception of God. We may conclude that Spinoza is throughout his career deeply interested to counter the effects of the misguided belief in the possibility of miracles.

For the sake of completeness we note that Spinoza follows this proof up with a tantalizing sketch of a second proof against the possibility of miracles. He writes that:

> The same thing can also easily be shown from the fact that the power of nature is the divine power and virtue itself, and the divine power is the very essence of God, but I am happy to leave this aside for the time being.
>
> (*TTP* 6.3)

As Spinoza puts this argument aside, we shall not dwell upon it. However, it is not difficult to reconstruct the basics of the proof that Spinoza has in mind. The argument would seem to go something like the following: Since God's power and the power of nature are one and the same, one cannot contradict the other. Thus, nothing can happen that is contrary to the power of nature, and if it did, it would entail a change in God's nature. Far from miracles proving the existence of an omnipotent (supernatural) deity, they would disprove it. It seems to us that we have here a hint of the much fuller metaphysical theory of the *Ethics*, which identifies God and Nature. We know that the composition of the *TTP* interrupted his work on the *Ethics*, so perhaps there is some "overlap" here. In any event, Spinoza decided not to add unneeded controversy into these important arguments, and so he did not pursue the issue further.

DEFENSE OF THE EPISTEMIC THESIS

Having argued that miracles cannot occur, Spinoza then proceeds to defend what we call the *Epistemic Thesis*. This is the claim "that from miracles we cannot know about either the essence or the existence or the providence of God, but rather that all three are

64 CRITIQUE OF TRADITIONAL BIBLICAL RELIGION

much better grasped from the fixed and unchanging order of nature" (*TTP* 6.2). Even if, *per impossibile*, miracles did exist, it would not affect religion because we could not infer anything about the nature of God from them. Spinoza provides three philosophical arguments for this claim and one Scriptural confirmation argument.

The first argument begins with Cartesian assumptions about knowledge. Spinoza writes that: "The existence of God is not known of itself, it must necessarily be deduced from concepts whose truth is so firm and unquestionable that no power capable of changing them can exist or be conceived" (*TTP* 6.6). This claim is at first surprising because Spinoza has claimed earlier (in his discussion of prophecy) that everyone has an idea of God. Perhaps to reconcile this contradiction Spinoza adds a note to this passage in the French edition which reads:

> As long as our idea of Him is confused, and not clear and distinct, we are in doubt about the existence of God, and consequently about everything. For just as someone who does not comprehend a triangle properly does not know that its three angles are equal to two right angles, so anyone with a confused conception of the divine nature does not see that it belongs to the nature of God to exist. In order to conceive the nature of God clearly and distinctly, we must take notice of certain very simple ideas that are called common notions and connect the things that belong to the divine nature with them.
>
> (*TTP* Annotation 6)

Spinoza is arguing in this section that miracles would not help one who had a confused or inadequate idea of God to get a clearer understanding of the divine. The only means by which one may come to know God, Spinoza thinks, is through a proof beginning with clear and distinct ideas. If one lacks such a proof, one will be in doubt about God. This doubt about God, Spinoza thinks, will lead to a general doubt about everything else. Spinoza clearly has in mind Descartes's arguments in the *Meditations*, that we must know God before we can know and understand anything else. Spinoza continues in a Cartesian vein: "For if we could conceive that the axioms themselves might be modified by whatever power, then we could doubt their truth, and hence also our conclusion

CRITIQUE OF TRADITIONAL BIBLICAL RELIGION 65

concerning God's existence, and could never be certain of anything" (*TTP* 6.6). The axioms upon which the proof of God's existence is inferred must be such that nothing could make them false. If it were possible for something somewhere to make these axioms false (while we take them to be true), then we could never be absolutely certain that they are in fact true. As a result, we could not be absolutely certain that God exists. Thus, for one who has a confused idea of God, the only way to come to know God is to deduce his existence from absolutely certain first principles. These principles are such as the Principle of Non-Contradiction (that no proposition p can be both true and false at the same time), the Principle of Sufficient Reason (that there is always an explanation for the existence or non-existence of a thing; see $E1p8s2$, $E1p11d2$), and the (analytic) truths of mathematics. Spinoza believes that these principles are innate to reason and so are known with absolute certainty. "We know," he continues, "that nothing conforms to nature or conflicts with it, except what we have shown to agree or conflict with these [evident] principles" (*TTP* 6.6). He clarifies his claim by asserting that "whatever is contrary to nature, is contrary to reason, and what is contrary to reason, is absurd, and accordingly to be rejected" (*TTP* 6.15). Thus, the only way to come to know God – for those who have a confused or inadequate idea of him – is to infer his existence on the basis of self-evident principles.

A genuine miracle, a real violation of the laws of nature, would conflict with these fundamental principles. Spinoza writes that:

If we could conceive that anything in nature could be brought about by any power (whatever that power might be) which conflicts with nature, it would be in conflict with those primary principles and therefore would have to be rejected as absurd, or else there would be doubts about those primary principles (as we have just shown) and, consequently, about God and all our perceptions of whatever kind.

(*TTP* 6.6)

A miracle would conflict with the fundamental ("primary") principles. Such an occurrence would be a significant epistemic problem because it would call into doubt these very fundamental principles, and hence the very possibility of knowledge of the existence of

66 CRITIQUE OF TRADITIONAL BIBLICAL RELIGION

God. Spinoza need not have a specific proof of God's existence in mind here. Whatever proof one chooses – Descartes's proof in the *Third Meditation*, classical Ontological Arguments, the Cosmological Argument, etc. – the proof will require certain principles to make the inference. If something occurred in nature, however, that violated these principles, that (miraculous) event would call reason and reasoned argument itself into doubt. And if reason were called into doubt, then no absolutely certain proofs could be offered for God's existence (or for anything else). Thus, on Spinoza's view, a miracle would make it impossible to prove the existence of God. Miracles "would make us call into doubt that very point [that God exists], since, without them, we could be absolutely certain of it, because we know that all things follow the certain and unchangeable order of nature" (*TTP* 6.6).

Spinoza's second argument for the Epistemic Thesis is short and simple. Spinoza writes that:

> Let it be supposed that a miracle is something that cannot be explained by natural causes ... It is a phenomenon that cannot be explained by a cause, that is, it is a phenomenon that surpasses human understanding. But we can understand nothing of a phenomenon, or of anything at all, that surpasses our understanding ... Therefore, we cannot understand from a miracle, or work which surpasses our understanding, the essence of God or his existence or anything about God and nature.
>
> (*TTP* 6.7)

If a miracle occurred, Spinoza argues, then it would surpass our understanding. But if it surpassed our understanding, then how could it teach us anything? According to Spinoza, one comes to know something either by directly grasping it with the intellect or by inferring it from absolutely certain propositions. Thus, commencing with something that one does not understand (such as a miracle), one cannot infer anything. The only way to infer the existence of God is to begin with premises that one *does* understand. Spinoza believes, like Aristotle, that we must begin with things that are better known and infer less-well-known things, not the other way around.

CRITIQUE OF TRADITIONAL BIBLICAL RELIGION 67

Spinoza's third argument for the Epistemic Thesis is equally simple. No matter how grand a miracle is, Spinoza argues, one could never infer that it was caused by an infinitely powerful being. Spinoza writes that:

> Even if we could draw conclusions from miracles, we certainly could not derive [from them] the existence of God. Given that a miracle is a limited phenomenon, and never reveals anything more than a fixed and limited power, it is certain that from such an effect we cannot infer the existence of a cause whose power is infinite, but at most a cause whose power is fairly large.
>
> *(TTP* 6.8)

This criticism will famously be repeated by Hume when offering a critique of the Cosmological Argument in Part IX of the *Dialogues Concerning Natural Religion.* Spinoza is certainly right in his claim that from a finite effect one cannot infer an infinite cause. Thus, from a miracle alone one cannot infer that God exists.

Spinoza believes that these three arguments are sufficient to prove the Epistemic Thesis. Nevertheless, he adds a Scriptural argument to the end of this section. "I should like," he writes, "to confirm my claim that we cannot achieve a knowledge of God from miracles with Scripture's authority" (*TTP* 6.10). It is interesting that he is seeking to confirm his previous philosophical arguments with Scriptural arguments. Spinoza's argument here reveals him to be intent on adapting his (radical) views to an audience that took arguments from Scripture very seriously. Spinoza begins this discussion in a surprising way by claiming that: "Even though Scripture nowhere explicitly tells us this [that miracles can teach us nothing about God], it may readily be inferred, especially from the command of Moses in Deuteronomy 13 to condemn a false prophet to death even if he performs miracles" (*TTP* 6.10). Because Scripture claims that *false* prophets can perform miracles, Spinoza infers, Scripture must likewise imply that miracles cannot themselves teach us about God. His point here seems to be that if miracles did provide evidence for the existence of God, then it would be impossible for a miracle to occur without an immediate inference to the existence of God. But the fact that miracles can occur and

68 CRITIQUE OF TRADITIONAL BIBLICAL RELIGION

yet one cannot validly infer truths about the existence of God (in the proffered Scriptural example of the false prophet) proves that miracles have no essential connection to God and his existence. Spinoza invokes the authority of Scripture in his case against miracles. Spinoza writes that:

> It is thus also evident from Scripture itself that miracles do not yield knowledge of God and do not clearly demonstrate the providence of God. The incidents frequently encountered in the Bible where God performs wonders to make himself known to men ... do not show that the miracles really prove this; they only show that the beliefs of the Jews were such that they could readily be convinced by these miracles.
>
> (*TTP* 6.11)

Using Scripture to draw conclusions that are antagonistic to traditional biblical religion is surely a provocative and innovative move. There have always been philosophers and critics of religion who have rejected traditional religious teachings, but only a few have dared to employ the Bible itself in their efforts. Spinoza had a traditional religious education, including textual analysis in the original biblical languages, before he rejected the tradition. He was unusually well positioned to evaluate the meaning of the Hebrew Bible in a way that was difficult for his contemporaries to resist.

DEFENSE OF THE SCRIPTURAL THESIS

The third thesis that Spinoza defends concerning miracles is what we call the *Scriptural Thesis*. This is the claim that "by decrees, volitions and providence of God, Scripture itself means nothing other than the order of nature which necessarily follows from his eternal law" (*TTP* 6.2). This argument is unlike the arguments from the previous two sections because it is not a philosophical argument, but an exegetical one. Spinoza makes this argument by means of examples. We will consider just three of Spinoza's examples. First, Spinoza takes a passage from Genesis 9:13 where "God informs Noah that he will put a rainbow in the clouds. This action of God's is

CRITIQUE OF TRADITIONAL BIBLICAL RELIGION 69

assuredly no other than the refraction and reflection affecting sun rays seen through drops of water" (*TTP* 6.13). Second, Spinoza tackles a passage from Psalms 105:24 which

> stated that God turned the hearts of the Egyptians to hate the Israelites; this too was a natural change, as emerges from the first chapter of Exodus which reports the urgent reason that motivated the Egyptians to reduce the Israelites to slavery.
>
> (*TTP* 6.13)

Third, Spinoza interprets a passage from 1 Samuel 9:15–16 which

> tells us that God revealed to Samuel that he would send Saul to him. But God did not send Saul to him as human beings are accustomed to send one man to another; this sending by God occurred simply according to the order of nature.
>
> (*TTP* 6.13)

In each of these passages Spinoza argues that the Bible is merely using "poetical" language to describe a natural event. There is nothing extraordinary and miraculous going on in these stories. In general, Spinoza's examples are drawn from the Hebrew Bible, not the New Testament. He does not for example choose to discuss the resurrection of Jesus, though in his letters he argues that the resurrection of Jesus should not be taken literally, but only "spiritually" (letter 75, to Oldenburg). Others who are "raised from the dead" by Jesus are taken to be "following him", accepting his holy teaching. After these exegeses Spinoza draws his general conclusion, namely, that:

> Without doubt, therefore, everything narrated in Scripture actually happened naturally, and yet it is all ascribed to God, since it is not the intention of the Bible, as we have shown, to explain things in terms of natural causes but only to speak of things that commonly occupy people's imaginations, and to do so in a manner and style calculated to inspire wonder about things and thus impress devotion upon the minds of the common people.
>
> (*TTP* 6.13)

70 CRITIQUE OF TRADITIONAL BIBLICAL RELIGION

Miracles exist only in the imagination of the common people. But this is just to say that there are no miracles upon reasoned reflection, once one discovers the natural cause of the event. What then is the role of the Bible for the community of believers? Is it a complete waste of time to study and live by it? More than almost anyone Spinoza believes that traditional religion infantilizes the believer and, worse, can incite him to violence and anarchy, all in the name of God. Nevertheless, Spinoza is enough of a realist about human nature, its frailties and limitations, that he believes that religion has a very important role, in fact a political role, to play in the state. And miracles are part of the story, as they can "impress devotion upon the minds of the common people" (*TTP* 6.13). Such teachings as traditional religion offers are amenable to political stability.

We have seen that Spinoza believes that miracles cannot occur, and even if they could, they could not ground religious belief in a supernatural divinity. Given this, one wonders whether Spinoza is being disingenuous in his interpretation that the Bible itself never actually claims to be relating supernatural events, but only natural events poetically described. We think not. As we will argue in the next chapter, Spinoza genuinely believes that religion, including its presentation of miraculous happenings, has a most important role to play in the State. Accordingly, he does not want to, indeed cannot, reject the Bible in its entirety. Rather he wishes to understand it in its own terms and then adapt it in accordance with his own theological-political understanding.

As we shall see, even though Spinoza will find a positive role for religion to play in the State, his critique of miracles is clearly intended to undermine the authority of the existing religious hierarchy. Seventeenth-century religious authorities (the Pope, the leaders of the Reformed Church, the rabbis) grounded their authority in a revelation confirmed by miracles ("signs"). Spinoza's arguments against miracles undercut their authority, and in so doing set the stage for a different role for religion in the modern state. Spinoza's arguments are not academic exercises for some obscure debating club, nor are they just brilliant displays of biblical scholarship. Rather they must be viewed as a direct challenge to the existing theological-political institutions. It is important when studying Spinoza's arguments to remember their very practical purpose.

CRITIQUE OF TRADITIONAL BIBLICAL RELIGION   71

CRITIQUE THREE: ON THE DIVINE LAW

We now turn to Spinoza's critique of the third foundation of traditional biblical religion, namely, the claim that the most important part of God's revelation to human beings by means of prophets concerns a set of rules, called the Divine Law, that when followed brings people closer to God. This law concerns a way of life that brings human beings closer to God. As finite beings, we could not have discovered the divine law on our own and so we needed God to tell us what it is. Spinoza begins his critique of this claim with some careful definitions. First, he defines law. He writes that:

> The word law (*lex*) in an absolute sense signifies that, in accordance with which, each individual thing, or all things, or all things of the same kind, behave in one and the same fixed and determined way, depending upon either natural necessity or a human decision. A law that depends upon natural necessity is one that necessarily follows from the very nature or definition of a thing.
>
> (*TTP* 4.1)

One of the common senses of "*lex*" concerns the physical laws that Spinoza believes follow from the nature of a thing. It is a natural physical law that cats meow, rabbits hop, and frogs eat flies. Each of these laws follows from the nature of these creatures. This sense of law is, however, not the primary sense of the word. Instead,

> [It] seems to be only by a metaphor that the word law (*lex*) is applied to natural things. What is commonly meant by a law is a command which men may or may not follow, since a law constrains human powers within certain limits which they naturally exceed ... Law therefore seems to have to be defined more precisely as "a rule for living which a man prescribes to himself or others for some purpose".
>
> (*TTP* 4.2)

In chapter four of the *Theological-Political Treatise* Spinoza is concerned primarily with law in this human sense, as one prescribed by human beings for other human beings. These "rules for living" differ not in their source, but in their purpose and trajectory. Spinoza notes that "the real purpose of laws is normally evident

72 CRITIQUE OF TRADITIONAL BIBLICAL RELIGION

only to a few" (*TTP* 4.2), with the result that most people will not know why they follow the rules that they do in fact follow. This "secularization" of law, whatever its purpose, is a counter to the claim that there is a third type of law, apart from the laws of nature and human laws, namely, divine commands of theistic natural law.

In chapter four of the *TTP* Spinoza begins his discussion of law by marking out two kinds of law: the laws of nature and human laws (*TTP* 4.1). These are the only two kinds of law that he believes exist. He defines a human law (*ius*) as "a rule for living which a man prescribes to himself or others for some purpose" (*TTP* 4.2). Human laws are then divided into two kinds, and are distinguished by their trajectory: those that aim simply "to protect life and preserve the country" (civil laws) and those that aim at the highest good (*TTP* 4.3). The first he calls "human laws" and the second "divine laws". Spinoza writes that, "by divine law I mean the law which looks only to the supreme good, that is, to the true knowledge and love of God" (*TTP* 4.3). Spinoza argues here (as he later does at the very end of the *Ethics*) that the supreme good of human beings, all human beings, is knowledge and love of God (or Nature).

It is important to note, once again, that Spinoza does not postulate a third kind of law – divine commands of theistic natural law – between the descriptive natural laws and human-made laws. For Spinoza, divine law is a species of human law, whose trajectory is the highest human good, the *summum bonum*. In this sense this species of human law is a natural law that accords with our (highest) human nature. Such a law allows human beings to flourish in the best possible way through acts of love and charity. These acts are grounded in "true knowledge and love of God" that go beyond mere protection of self and preservation of country. Spinoza's great predecessor in the medieval Jewish philosophical tradition, Maimonides, held precisely the same view about the twin goals of (the) law – protection of life and knowledge of God – even though Maimonides held its origin to be divine, a view that Spinoza, of course, rejects (*Guide of the Perplexed* 3.27).

Spinoza's claim about the highest good and the ultimate goal of the law, knowledge of God, is of interest here because Spinoza offers at least three ways to interpret and defend

CRITIQUE OF TRADITIONAL BIBLICAL RELIGION **73**

the claim that the supreme good of human beings is knowledge and love of God:

> Since all our knowledge and the certainty which truly takes away all doubt depends on a knowledge of God alone, and since without God nothing can exist or be conceived, and since we are in doubt about everything as long as we have no clear and distinct idea of God, it follows that our highest good and perfection depends upon a knowledge of God.

> (*TTP* 4.4)

Philosophically inclined readers (such as Spinoza's inner circle of friends) will see a Cartesian point here and remember arguments from the *Meditations*. The highest good is to know God because without this knowledge one cannot escape radical skepticism. Strict Spinozists will go a step further than this when they read the defense of knowledge of God as the ultimate aim of the law. Attentive to Spinoza's technical terminology from the *Ethics*, Spinoza's claim about the *summum bonum* will be for them a claim that the highest human good is a deep understanding of Nature and the laws that govern it. As noted, Spinoza is writing for a variety of audiences, each of whom will understand in a certain way the claim that knowledge of God is the *summum bonum*. When Spinoza asserts that the highest good is knowledge of God, this claim will seem to the common person to be a familiar religious platitude, perhaps enjoining deep devotion and obedience; to the Cartesian, it will appear as a foundational claim for resolving hyperbolic doubt; and finally to the Spinozist, who identifies God and Nature, knowledge of God is knowledge of basic metaphysics and natural science. These arguments concerning the *summum bonum* serve as a good example of the strategic ambiguity that Spinoza uses so carefully. Spinoza concludes this passage by claiming that:

> This then is what our highest good and happiness is, the knowledge and love of God. Therefore the means required by this end of all human actions, which is God himself so far as his idea is in us, may be called the commands of God, because they are prescribed to us,

74 CRITIQUE OF TRADITIONAL BIBLICAL RELIGION

> as it were, by God himself in so far as he exists in our minds, and therefore the rule of life which looks to this end is called the divine law.
>
> (*TTP* 4.4)

Strikingly, Spinoza claims here that "the commands of God" (the divine law) are nothing but the idea of God in each of us. From this idea of God, whether the inadequate idea of the common person, the Cartesian, or the Spinozist, we can infer that the highest good of human life is to know God, and "the rule of life which looks to this end is called the divine law". As we make intellectual progress, Spinoza believes we may eventually reach a fully adequate idea of God as Nature, as he expounds in the *Ethics*, and proceed to live our lives in accordance with this understanding. Short of this, the general rules of life can still be inferred from the inadequate conception of God of the common person. Though the common person follows the law without an adequate understanding of its trajectory, Spinoza hopes that in the right kind of social and political setting this individual will be able to live a life at least not rent asunder by religious strife and superstition.

Spinoza draws at least four consequences from this conception of the divine law. First, Spinoza infers that the divine law is "universal or common to all men" (*TTP* 4.6). This claim strikes at the heart of his ancestral Jewish community. The Judaism and the Jewish community in which Spinoza was raised firmly believed that Jews were specifically chosen by God and given a unique divine law (the Torah). Their self-identity involved seeing themselves as the guardians of this unique law and tradition. Spinoza rejects this view completely by claiming that the teachings of the divine law can be inferred from anyone's understanding of God, although of course the less adequate the understanding of God, the less adequate the understanding of the trajectory of the divine law. Second, Spinoza infers that the divine law "does not require belief in any kind of historical narrative" (*TTP* 4.6). Knowledge of the divine law (the laws for good living) is innate: all human beings possess it and it is not inculcated by an historical examination or narrative of a venerable figure. The life of such a person can serve as nothing more than an example. Living according to the divine

CRITIQUE OF TRADITIONAL BIBLICAL RELIGION 75

law is not a parochial enterprise. Third, Spinoza concludes that "the natural divine law does not require ceremonies" (*TTP* 4.6). Religious ceremonies may have social functions and purposes, but they have no *moral* purpose. Ceremonies and religious rituals by themselves mean nothing. Fourth and finally, "the supreme reward of the divine law is to know the law itself, that is, to know God and to love him in true liberty with whole and constant minds" (*TTP* 4.6). The true reward of the divine law is to live it, and so to live the best kind of life. There is nothing more to it than that. Living the divine law is not itself a means to a further end or reward (communion with God or eternal life). Rather for Spinoza, living in accord with the divine law is just to live the best kind of human life.

These inferences are radical in their implications. If the divine law, which is necessary for human happiness, is (a) universal, (b) requires no knowledge of history, (c) requires no ceremonies, and (d) has no purpose other than to live the best kind of life, then traditional biblical religion and the life enjoined by it is fundamentally in error. Traditional religion, with its rule following and ceremonial pomp, is quite unnecessary for a good life.

Spinoza attempts to defend his interpretation of the divine law through a study of the Scriptures. He begins his discussion by reminding us of the previous distinction made between the imagination (which concerns images and is always inadequate) and the intellect (which does not concern images and is always adequate). The laws of nature (the "eternal laws of God") can be known in one of two ways, either by means of the imagination or by means of the intellect. It is in this context that Spinoza considers the story of the Fall of Adam and Eve in Genesis. He writes, "we must necessarily infer that God [in enjoining Adam not to eat the fruit] only revealed to Adam the bad effects that would necessarily befall him if he ate of the tree" (*TTP* 4.9). God ordered Adam and Eve not to eat from the tree and grounded his command in the dire (natural) consequences that would accrue to Adam and to his offspring. God spoke to Adam as he did because Adam (humankind) was not yet capable of understanding the law as an eternal truth. Spinoza continues:

76 CRITIQUE OF TRADITIONAL BIBLICAL RELIGION

> This is how it was that Adam perceived that revelation not as an eternal and necessary truth but rather as a ruling, that is, as a convention that gain or loss follows not from the necessity and nature of the action done, but only from the pleasure and absolute command of the prince. Therefore that revelation was a law and God was a kind of legislator or prince exclusively with respect to Adam, and only because of the deficiency of his knowledge.
>
> *(TTP* 4.9)

It is hardly surprising, therefore, that after Adam ate the apple, he *imagined* that the pain and suffering that accrued were a punishment for violating the command of God. Adam understood God as a kind of legislator who issues arbitrary orders and causes pain to those who do not obey orders. This (consequentialist) imagining of the situation is completely inadequate from the point of view of the *summum bonum*, knowledge of God, that Spinoza has previously outlined. Without the requisite knowledge of the natural order, Adam cannot fully understand what is happening to him, and why. He perceives the situation through the prism of the imagination, and as a result God is viewed as a lord or king.

This way of thinking about the laws of nature and the divine law is not unique to Adam and did not end with him. Spinoza asserts that since the Jews "did not know the existence of God as an eternal truth, i.e., that God exists and that God alone is to be adored, they had to understand it [the law] as a decree" (*TTP* 4.9). The institutionalization of religion, and the rule following that governs it, leads us astray from the true goal of life and the "eternal truth" of loving one's neighbor and seeking knowledge for its own sake. We should not conclude from this narrative that Spinoza thinks that Scripture is useless or simply a repository of arcane history. In fact Spinoza holds that Scripture does not teach anything contrary to his own view that the divine law is universal, non-historical, non-ceremonial, and done for its own sake. Rather, Scripture speaks in terms of the imagination for understandable reasons, given its audience, explains natural events in inadequate ways, and presents a universal moral message in a parochial form. For Spinoza, the biblical narratives of the

CRITIQUE OF TRADITIONAL BIBLICAL RELIGION **77**

Israelites are extremely important. They are cautionary tales, case studies of human nature and the effects of superstition and fantastical thinking. But the core universal message of Scripture, the divine law, is revealed if one "abstracts" it from its "imaginative" shell.

The immediate *political* relevance of these claims about the universality of the divine law is clear. If the divine law is not unique to one religious faith or one set of revelations, and if it is available to all, then a "catholic" religion is a possibility, one that does not pit one group against another. Such a universal religion might even be a foundation for social stability, given the inclusivity of its message.

CRITIQUE FOUR: ON THE INTERPRETATION OF SCRIPTURE

The fourth foundation of traditional biblical religion as Spinoza understood it is the claim that the divine law can be found by interpreting Scripture. Scripture is the Word of God and so is infallible. The early modern debates over the correct way to interpret the Bible are without doubt a watershed in European history. To put it perhaps too simply, this hermeneutical issue *is* the Protestant Reformation. Martin Luther's critiques of the Church and its hegemony in the sixteenth century were still dividing Europe in the seventeenth century. Political questions quickly became entangled in religious questions, often over who had the sovereign right to interpret the Scriptures. Some radical Protestants argued that anyone, not just the Church authorities, could read the Bible for him- or herself and understand it. No special training was required. The Holy Spirit on this view is quite egalitarian. When reading the Bible, God could in some sense speak directly to the individual reader (through the Holy Spirit) and converse with him or her. By contrast, the Catholic Church argued that it took individuals trained in the original languages and the history of theological debates over the centuries to understand and interpret the Bible correctly. A layman who read the Bible for himself was, the Church argued, likely to misunderstand it without such a rigorous education.

78 CRITIQUE OF TRADITIONAL BIBLICAL RELIGION

Apart from these two opposing positions, a host of others were offered, including a controversial suggestion that natural philosophy (science) was key to the interpretation of Scripture. This view was offered by one of Spinoza's close friends, Lodewijk Meyer.

In 1633 Galileo was put on trial by the Church not, as is often believed, for claiming that the earth moves around the sun. Rather, what upset the Catholic bishops was Galileo's claim that, given these astronomical truths, we should interpret certain passages in Joshua 10:13 concerning the sun stopping in the sky as speaking in human terms, grounded in a non-scientific, imaginative outlook. What Scripture really means is that the earth stopped moving on its axis for some short time. This may seem like a minor point, but in a time of shifting powers and growing skepticism about traditional authority, such a claim was considered dangerous because it seemed to suggest that individuals other than Catholic bishops had the right to interpret Scripture authoritatively. Following Luther's condemnation of the Church, a claim such as that of Galileo was not surprisingly seen as having dangerous political implications. The real question at issue was not the truth of the emerging science, but rather who had religious and political authority.

In this context Spinoza's discussion of the interpretation of Scripture is bold to the point of recklessness. Spinoza begins his discussion by condemning both laypeople and theologians (of all denominations) for their interpretations of Scripture. He writes:

> All men are ready to say that Holy Scripture is the word of God that teaches us true happiness or the way of salvation, but their actions betray a quite different opinion. For the common people, the last thing that they appear to want is to live by the teaching of Scripture. We see them advancing false notions of their own as the word of God and seeking to use the influence of religion to compel other people to agree with them. As for theologians, we see that forthe most part they have sought to extract their own thoughts and opinions from the Bible and thereby endow them with divine authority.

(*TTP* 7.1)

CRITIQUE OF TRADITIONAL BIBLICAL RELIGION 79

Spinoza claims in this section that it is personal ambition and the vainglorious desire to be original that distorts interpretations of the Bible. Everyone, Spinoza thinks, seeks to read into the Scriptures his or her own ideas and so gain divine sanction for them. Given the ambiguous nature of the text, it is possible to read into it a great many things, with the result that, human nature being what it is, "vice and ambition have in the end exercised so much influence that religion has been made to consist in defending purely human delusions rather than following the teachings of the Holy Spirit" (*TTP* 7.1). The personal ambition of religious leaders has so distorted the truth of the Scriptural message that the traditional biblical teachings are nothing more than "human delusions". The simple, true moral teachings are lost. This (Protestant-like) claim of returning to basics was a popular one among radical religious reformers in the seventeenth century, and in fact would become even more prominent over the next two centuries as liberal theologians sought to remove centuries of corruption and obfuscation in order to unearth the original message embedded in Scripture. Spinoza's discussion is a touchstone for these reformers and his foundational work in Scriptural hermeneutics was widely debated into the nineteenth century.

Spinoza commences to defend his own hermeneutical views by claiming that:

> I hold that the method of interpreting Scripture does not differ from the method of interpreting nature, but rather is wholly consonant with it. The method of interpreting nature consists above all in constructing a natural history, from which we derive the definitions of natural things, as from certain data. Likewise, to interpret Scripture, we need to assemble a genuine history of it and to deduce the thinking of the Bible's authors by valid inferences from this history, as from certain data and principles.
>
> (*TTP* 7.2)

Spinoza demands a "scientific" approach to the study of the Bible. He suggests that we ought to examine the text in just the way that we would examine an interesting stone or tree, by

80 CRITIQUE OF TRADITIONAL BIBLICAL RELIGION

collecting data, inspecting the surrounding environment carefully, not jumping to conclusions, etc. Spinoza believes that this method of understanding Scripture will be more "objective" than the regnant methods, precisely because it will seek to understand the Bible in its own terms and not attempt to read into the Bible preconceived notions. After all, much of what occurs in Scripture is historical narrative, adapted to the understandings of different audiences at different times. We need first to understand the Bible by understanding what it actually says and precisely how it conveys its message, and then try to ascertain what it actually meant to these early audiences. Only then can we assess the truth of what is asserted. Spinoza views Scripture as an historical text like any other, and thus one that may be studied by means of a dispassionate and scientific approach. Any critical evaluation that might be made must be founded on such a careful analysis.

Spinoza's two-step procedure of first interpreting and then assessing the truth of what is said stands in sharp contrast to almost all the theologians and philosophers of his day. Spinoza does not begin with the assumption that what is written in Scripture – even when properly interpreted – is true. Scripture is not inerrant. It is a book like any other. Spinoza is not straightaway concerned with uncovering truths, but rather is concerned with understanding the full context of the text itself. For Spinoza, one should seek to understand Scripture first and only then assess whether what is said is in fact true, or not. Scriptural revelation must not lull our critical, even skeptical, sensibilities. It could in fact turn out that Scripture may stand in opposition to the truths of modern science. The Bible, a work of considerable age, might unsurprisingly presuppose proto-scientific truths that we now know to be false. If Aristotle could become outdated, why not the Bible?

For an instructive comparison, consider the view of Lodewijk Meyer, Spinoza's close friend and fellow radical, whose views Spinoza very likely had in mind when he was working on the *Tractatus*. In his controversial and universally condemned work *Philosophy as the Interpreter of Holy Scripture* (1666) Meyer writes that:

CRITIQUE OF TRADITIONAL BIBLICAL RELIGION   81

> The true interpreter of the Holy Writings is one who can elicit the truths of the sentences therein contained and show that he has done so ... Philosophy is the true, certain, and indubitable knowledge of things, deduced from principles known by the natural light and logically demonstrated ... From this it most evidently follows that philosophy is the sure and infallible norm both for interpreting the Holy Writings and for examining interpretations.
>
> *(Philosophy as the Interpreter of Holy Scripture*, p. 113)

By "philosophy" Meyer includes natural science. Thus, Meyer is arguing that natural science is the true rule ("norm") for the interpretation and evaluation of Scripture. Meyer's argument for this conclusion is straightforward. He argues first that Scripture is the Word of God and so is inerrant. Then he argues that the truths we know from natural science are indubitable. Thus, he infers, we must interpret Scripture in such a way that all that is written in it conforms to the truths of natural science. For Meyer, like Averroes, "truth is not opposed to truth". When there is a *prima facie* disputed passage (for example, the passage in Joshua about the stopping of the sun), we should interpret it in light of what we know to be indubitably true from natural science.

Spinoza roundly rejects Meyer's method because Spinoza does not presume as a starting point that all that is written in Scripture is true, and further because he does not, like Meyer, think that philosophy and science are the keys that unlock the meaning of the texts. For Spinoza, as we have seen, it is rather historical and philological analyses that are the tools for interpreting Scripture. Spinoza argues that: "if we want to attest the divine character of Scripture objectively, we must establish from the Bible alone that it offers true moral doctrines. This is the only ground on which its divine character can be proven" (*TTP* 7.4). We need first to understand the text in a most painstaking way, taking into account all contexts, and only after we have done so will we be in a position to evaluate its moral doctrines, the Word of God. "The universal rule then for interpreting Scripture," Spinoza argues, "is to claim nothing as biblical doctrine that we have not derived, by the closest possible scrutiny, from its own [the Bible's] history" (*TTP* 7.5). And how exactly will we be able finally to *evaluate* the

82 CRITIQUE OF TRADITIONAL BIBLICAL RELIGION

moral doctrines that we find in the Bible? Not surprisingly, on the basis of reason. The moral message is not true because of divine authority or institutional decree. If the teachings accord with the divine laws given by the natural light of reason, then what is written in the Bible is true. If not, then what is written in the Bible is false, though understandable in its historical context and even pedagogically useful.

Spinoza's scientific-historical method of biblical interpretation raises, once again, the issue of his intended audience. For whom is Spinoza writing? Clearly he is not writing for the traditional religious (Church) authorities or those common people who follow the religious authorities. Both groups would immediately reject his starting assumptions that the text has no authoritative status and must be subjected to the same analysis that historical texts receive. From the vantage point of his Scriptural hermeneutics, it appears that Spinoza's intended audience would be other like-minded radical "freethinkers". But if his target group is a small band of freethinkers, why was the text greeted with such widespread outrage upon its appearance in 1670? Clearly the book was read by more people than just a few like-minded radicals. There appears to be a significant disconnect between the trajectory of the project and its intended audience. Spinoza seems to want to change society with his book and at the same time he appears to aim the *TTP* at a small and politically insignificant circle.

In the Preface to the *TTP* Spinoza tells us explicitly whom he considers his audience to be. He says that he wrote the book for the "philosophical reader" and that "the main points are well enough known to philosophers" (*TTP* pref. 15). He then goes on to say that

> As for others, I am not particularly eager to recommend this treatise to them, for I have no reason to expect that it could please them in any way. I know how obstinately those prejudices stick in the mind that the heart has embraced in the form of piety.
>
> (*TTP*, pref. 15)

Spinoza seems to have in mind with these remarks that the *TTP* will be read by "unprejudiced" philosophical types who would be current

CRITIQUE OF TRADITIONAL BIBLICAL RELIGION 83

with ongoing developments in natural science. This gives the *TTP* a rather cosmopolitan feel, and perhaps also explains why the harsh criticism came from all quarters, both religious and political. Perhaps Spinoza hoped that through his intended ("enlightened") audience a seed of rationality might grow into a movement (the Enlightenment) for an understanding of religion that would allow for the ongoing development of science as well as the stabilizing of the political community by a harmonizing of divisive, sectarian concerns. Perhaps the most we can say is that he was searching for an (unprejudiced) audience that had both a keen sense of the harm that traditional religion has wrought, and a sense of the role it might play, properly reformed, in the modern world, an increasingly secular world.

To return now to Spinoza's argument, he argues that to begin to understand Scripture one needs a "history of the Scriptures". Such a history has three parts. First, "such a history must include the nature and properties of the language in which the biblical books were composed" (*TTP* 7.5). If we are to understand Scripture, we first need a fluency in the languages in which the texts were originally composed. Second, the history "must gather together the opinions expressed in each individual book and organize them by subject so that we may have available by this means all the statements that are found on each topic" (*TTP* 7.5). This second step in creating a history of the Scriptures is analogous to collecting specimens in a biology laboratory. If one wishes to know what a certain word or phrase means, then one should look at all of the other uses of that word or phrase. Only after they have been compiled and checked against each other, is it possible to glean the general meaning that these expressions have. Third, Spinoza argues that:

Our historical inquiry must explain the circumstances of all the books of the prophets whose memory has come down to us: the life, character and particular interests of the author of each individual book, who exactly he was, on what occasion he wrote, for whom and in what language. Then the fate of each book: namely, how it was first received and whose hands it came into, how many variant readings there have been of its text, by whose decision it was received among

84 CRITIQUE OF TRADITIONAL BIBLICAL RELIGION

> the sacred books, and finally how all the books which are now accepted as sacred came to form a single corpus.
>
> (*TTP* 7.5)

We must know both the circumstances in which the texts were written as well as the means by which they were transmitted to us. Spinoza is on the lookout for later accretions that might have infected the original. Spinoza thinks that understanding the circumstances of composition is particularly important because only when we know this will we be able to "know which statements are meant as laws and which are moral doctrine" (*TTP* 7.5). Only by examining the circumstances of composition (and the general prejudices of the time) will we be able to ascertain which parts of Scripture convey universal moral truths and which parts are parochialisms adapted for specific historical circumstances. Once this is resolved, the adaptions can then be set to one side, leaving only the moral truths (the divine laws) in need of examination for their veracity.

When this history has been compiled, one may commence the scientific study of Scripture by exploring the "most universal and common" things and working our way down to the more specific things (*TTP* 7.6). The common and universal teaching of Scripture on Spinoza's view is that:

> There is a God, one and omnipotent, who alone is to be adored and cares for all men, loving most those who worship Him and love their neighbor as themselves, etc. ... But Scripture does not teach expressly, as eternal doctrine, what God is, and how he sees all things and provides for them, and so on.
>
> (*TTP* 7.6)

Spinoza argues that such moral ideas concerning divine beneficence and love are to be noted repeatedly and consistently throughout the Scriptures, both in the Hebrew and the Greek texts, and, as we shall see in chapter five, these ideas form the core of his Universal Religion. Once we isolate and identify these universal teachings we can then turn to the specific teachings which flow "like rivulets from the universal teaching" (*TTP* 7.7). Spinoza

CRITIQUE OF TRADITIONAL BIBLICAL RELIGION 85

considers a number of specific examples. Here we pick only one particularly interesting issue: the relationship between the teaching of Moses and that of Jesus. Concerning this question, Spinoza writes that

> Moses (who did not write at a time of oppression, but, it should be noticed, was striving to construct a well-ordered state) issued the edicts to pay an eye for an eye, even though he too condemned vengeance and hatred of one's neighbor. Thus, it most evidently follows from the very principles of Scripture itself, that the doctrine of suffering injury and giving way to impious men in everything [as Jesus taught], is appropriate only in places where justice is neglected and in times of oppression, but not in a well-ordered state.
>
> (*TTP* 7.7)

Here is a clear example of how an understanding of the circumstances surrounding the composition of Scripture can help the reader to interpret the text. Once we understand the different circumstances and the different purposes (Moses' political, state-constructing agenda and Jesus' moral-reforming agenda), we can see that these two teachers and leaders are not actually contradicting each other. Jesus' teachings do not replace Moses', on Spinoza's view; instead they each apply the same principle of loving one's neighbor to different social and political settings.

Spinoza then turns to a much more difficult issue: the *philosophical* teachings of the different biblical authors. Concerning this Spinoza begins

> But other matters to be found in the Bible concerning purely philosophical questions, cannot be so easily resolved. The path to be followed here is more arduous. As we have seen, the prophets disagreed among themselves in philosophical matters, and their narratives of things are very much adapted to the presuppositions of their respective times, and therefore we may not infer or explain the meaning of one prophet from clearer passages in another, unless it is absolutely evident that they both held the same opinion.
>
> (*TTP* 7.8)

86 CRITIQUE OF TRADITIONAL BIBLICAL RELIGION

Two features make understanding the philosophical (universal) teachings of the biblical authors difficult. First, as we have noted, the prophetic message is indexed to the specific beliefs of each individual prophet. One cannot presuppose that their respective messages are the same, or even consistent. There is no one prophetic message that all the prophets are delivering. Thus, to understand the true teachings, the real views, of each of the prophets, one must separate the incidental accretions due to time and circumstance. Second, we cannot use passages from other books of the Bible to shed light on obscure passages, unless we have very good reason to think that they can be compared. Otherwise it would be like comparing apples and oranges. Given the very different philosophical presentations about God that Scripture offers, one must take each author in isolation. Given the lack of reliable and detailed historical information, therefore, Spinoza believes that it is almost impossible to identify the philosophical views of the individual prophets in many cases.

After employing his method to reach some interesting conclusions concerning the consistency of the moral teachings in the Bible and the divergent philosophical teachings, Spinoza notes three significant limitations to his method. First, "a major obstacle in this method is that it requires a perfect knowledge of the Hebrew language" (*TTP* 7.11). Such knowledge, Spinoza believes, is almost impossible because there were no native Hebrew speakers in his day. Among other problems, "almost all the names of fruits, birds, fish, and very many other words, have perished through the ravages of time" (*TTP* 7.11). Spinoza himself attempted to help remedy this situation by beginning to write a Hebrew grammar. But even he could not translate some obscure passages in Scripture (most notably passages from the book of Job). This fact is a serious limitation in our attempts to understand accurately what the texts really mean.

A second major limitation is that this method "requires a history of the vicissitudes of all the biblical books, and most of this is unknown to us" (*TTP* 7.15). To know how the books may have been modified during their long history, a complete transmission history would be required. This is an impossible task. Virtually all of the

CRITIQUE OF TRADITIONAL BIBLICAL RELIGION **87**

redactors of the Scriptures throughout the centuries are entirely unknown to us. What motives they may have had when transmitting Scripture remains and will remain a mystery. We can never know, therefore, what the "autographs" looked like. Even if we accepted (as Spinoza's contemporaries did) that the "autograph" versions of the biblical books represent the literal Word of God, we could not now know what those texts actually looked like. This will always leave us with considerable uncertainty regarding the actual contents and meaning of these books.

A third major limitation that Spinoza notes is that "we do not now have them [the Scriptures] in the same language in which they were originally written. The Gospel of Matthew and without doubt the Letter to the Hebrews are commonly believed to have been composed in Hebrew, but these versions are not extant" (*TTP* 7.16). The earliest manuscripts that we have are the Greek editions of the New Testament. Whether there were earlier Hebrew or Aramaic editions is unknown to us. This fact leaves us even another step removed from the "autograph" originals of the biblical texts.

Given these limitations to the scientific approach to Scripture, Spinoza concludes that "I think these difficulties are so great that I do not hesitate to affirm that in numerous passages either we do not know the true sense of Scripture or can only guess at it without any assurance" (*TTP* 7.17). In the final analysis, one must confess that very often one cannot know what Scripture actually means. Our ignorance, however, is not total. For Spinoza continues that, nevertheless,

> we can readily discover the meaning of the Bible's moral teaching from the history of it that we are able to reconstruct, and can be certain about its true sense. For the teachings of true piety are expressed in the most everyday language, since they are very common and extremely simple and easy to understand.
>
> (*TTP* 7.17)

While we can never be certain about the meaning of philosophical teachings we find in Scripture, we can identify the *moral*

88 CRITIQUE OF TRADITIONAL BIBLICAL RELIGION

teachings and further, we can verify the truth of them by the natural light of reason.

The real political relevance of Spinoza's views on the interpretation of Scripture emerges clearly at the end of chapter seven of the *TTP* where he writes that:

> In case anyone is misled by the example of the Hebrew High Priest to believe that the Catholic religion too requires a high priest, one must remark that the laws of Moses were the public laws of a country and necessarily needed therefore a public authority for their preservation. If every individual had the liberty to interpret the public laws at his own discretion, no state could survive ... It is wholly different with religion. Since it does not consist so much in external actions as in simplicity and truth of mind, it does not belong to any public law or authority ... Absolutely no one can be compelled to be happy by force of law.
>
> *(TTP* 7.22)

Institutional religion, Spinoza claims, makes a fundamental error in its attempt to establish religious authority in the State. It confounds the political and legal teachings of Moses with the religious and moral teachings of Jesus. The political teachings of Moses are relevant only in a Jewish state. Once the distinction between religion and politics, between actions and inner piety, is made, Spinoza believes that the case for an "executive" role for the Church and institutional religion in political life collapses. True religion, Spinoza argues, "does not consist so much in external actions as in simplicity and truth of mind, it does not belong to any public law or authority" (*TTP* 7.22). If a new understanding of the Scriptures, such as the one Spinoza offers, were to take hold, one that searches for common ground and sees differences due to historical circumstance as unimportant, then there might be hope for a lessening of the political instability that was everywhere to be seen. A scientific study of Scripture undercuts the apologetic thrust of institutional religion and thereby the (political) authority of those that rely on it. With such an intellectual "revolution", and perhaps we should

CRITIQUE OF TRADITIONAL BIBLICAL RELIGION 89

understand the *Theological-Political Treatise* as its manifesto, the hope is that much of the causes of religious conflict will fade away.

CONCLUSION

Spinoza rejected all four of the foundations of traditional biblical religion. First, he argued that the prophets were individuals with vivid imaginations, no more and no less. Such moral truths that they taught are not supernatural truths, as they may be confirmed by the natural light of reason. Contrary to traditional teachings, God does not speak to human beings uniquely through prophetic revelation. The role of the prophet for Spinoza is political and pedagogical, for the prophet through his imaginative capacities can instruct the masses on how best to live. Second, Spinoza argued that miracles are impossible and would teach us nothing about God, even if they were possible. A religion founded on miracles is, therefore, fundamentally mistaken. Third, he argued that the divine law, the directives for living a good life, are available to everyone by means of the natural light of reason. They are universal and require no ceremonies or knowledge of religious history. Fourth, Spinoza argued that Scripture consists of true moral beliefs adapted to the (often primitive) understandings of different peoples at different times. Spinoza treats Scripture as an historical artifact, something to be studied in a manner analogous to the study of any natural organism. Sensitive analysis requires study of the original languages, cultures, and lives of the authors. Only through such study can we hope to recover the true meaning of Scripture. The universalizing and democratizing implications of Spinoza's biblical critique have the effect of undercutting the political authority of institutional religion, and thus aid in overcoming factionalism and enhancing political stability in the State.

FURTHER READING

For context and historical background to Spinoza's critique of biblical religion, see Preus (2001) and Popkin (1996). For a general discussion of *TTP*, chapters 1–7, where Spinoza presents his ("naturalist") views on prophecy and the prophets, miracles, divine law, and the interpretation of Scripture, see Nadler (2007 and 2011, chapters 4–6) and James (2012, chapters 2–7). Curley (1994) discusses Spinoza's biblical hermeneutics, and Rutherford (2010) discusses divine law and natural rights.

5

THE UNIVERSAL RELIGION

INTRODUCTION

Spinoza argues that traditional biblical religion as institutionalized by the Church should not be the basis of political life because it is false, grounded in superstition, and divisive. These determinations about traditional biblical religion have a number of important political consequences. In this chapter and the next we examine these consequences. Perhaps surprisingly, Spinoza does not conclude that we should outlaw or abolish traditional biblical religion. Spinoza is a realist about human nature and a pragmatist about the abiding role of religion in political life. He argues that, properly understood and institutionally reformed, religion can and should be incorporated into the political structures of the state. We emphasize that his goal is to *revise* the role that religion plays in politics, not to eliminate it. Religion, properly understood, can be an instrument in enhancing social stability. This new role that religion will play in Spinoza's vision of modern political life is quite different from the role that it plays in the Christendom Model.

92 THE UNIVERSAL RELIGION

The main result of Spinoza's critique of religion is to undercut the status of the Church in relation to the political authority. The Church does not give any kind of authority or legitimacy to the sovereign; on the contrary, "authority in sacred matters belongs wholly to the sovereign [political] powers" (*TTP* 19, title). The Church in an ideal state, as Spinoza envisions it, would derive whatever authority it had from the authority of the sovereign political power. This subordination of Church authority to the authority of the State, however, is limited to *external* religion and does not concern *internal* religion. This distinction is the central distinction needed to understand the new role that Spinoza thinks religion should play in the state. External religion concerns actions – whether people act obediently, justly, and charitably, along with whatever beliefs are necessary for living such a life. Internal religion concerns dogmatic metaphysical beliefs about the nature of God, the immortality of the soul, the existence of heaven and hell, etc. Everyone has total freedom – as we will see in the next chapter – to determine internal religious matters for herself without interference from the State. This freedom presupposes, however, that each citizen is living within the parameters of the external religion, that is, as long as she is obedient to the civil laws, just, and charitable. Spinoza thus argues for a total subordination of religion to political authority in external matters along with a total freedom of religion in internal matters. Whether Spinoza's views are viable turns primarily on whether internal religion can be so entirely separated from external religion in the way that Spinoza demands. This chapter concerns Spinoza's external religion. We will examine his case for the freedom of internal religion (and with it scientific and philosophical matters) in the next chapter.

We begin this chapter by examining how Spinoza distinguishes between external and internal religion. We then examine in some detail Spinoza's Universal Religion or public faith. This public faith, grounded in the universal truths culled from his interpretation of Scripture, is the set of beliefs that are necessary for living a life that is obedient, just, and charitable. We will pay particular attention to whether this religion is broad enough to include Spinoza himself, since he demands that *everyone* in the state must accept this Universal Religion. After considering each

THE UNIVERSAL RELIGION 93

of the dogmas in turn we conclude that Spinoza is sufficiently flexible that even atheists could accept the Universal Religion that Spinoza outlines in chapter 14 of the *Theological-Political Treatise*.

SEPARATING INTERNAL RELIGIOUS BELIEFS FROM EXTERNAL RELIGIOUS PRACTICES

Given Spinoza's radical rejection of traditional biblical religion, why not simply abandon religion *in toto*? Why not argue for a truly secular state where religion plays no political role at all? There are at least three reasons that keep Spinoza from calling for an end to all religious observance and practice in the ideal republic. First, such a recommendation would be quite unreasonable in Spinoza's day (or indeed even today). The overwhelming majority were deeply religious and regular churchgoers. To call for the abandonment of all religion would have been practically impossible and hopelessly idealistic. It bears repeating that it is important to keep in mind how very much a student of human nature Spinoza is. Furthermore, a proposal to eliminate religion and religious observance would have marginalized Spinoza's work even more than it already was. If Spinoza's political views were going to have any immediate success at all (and of course they did not!), then they would need to appeal to more than his small circle of philosophical "freethinkers", who themselves might even understand the need for religion, properly reformed, in the modern state. A second reason that keeps Spinoza from calling for an end to all religious observance is the felt need to find some common ground, a shared consensus, to ensure that peaceful resolution of conflict is possible. Although Spinoza believes that the common ground needed for political stability is small ("thin"), it is not so thin as to allow total diversity of opinion about everything. He believes that certain value parameters must be established to secure proper civic behavior. Spinoza believes that religion, properly adapted and controlled, will be helpful in this regard. As a result, distinguishing a common (religious) ground from contentious religious questions is one of Spinoza's major tasks in his political philosophy. Finally, and closely linked to the foregoing, we may discern a third reason that prevents Spinoza from calling for an

94 THE UNIVERSAL RELIGION

end to all religious observance. He needs a "mechanism" for the cultivation of certain liberal virtues (such as tolerance), which themselves are required for the functioning of a peaceful republic. Spinoza believes that, properly reformed, individual churches can be of real value to the state by cultivating those necessary civic virtues in their parishioners. The challenge, as Spinoza sees it, is to convince the existing religious institutions to cultivate the necessary civic virtues without thereby dividing the republic along religious lines. Spinoza's solution is to separate external from internal religion.

Spinoza defends the distinction between internal and external religion on the basis of his analysis of the Bible. Spinoza begins his discussion by saying

> Let us restate the supreme purpose of the whole of the Bible, for that will guide us to the true criterion for defining faith. We said in the last chapter that the sole aim of Scripture is to teach obedience. This no one can contest.
>
> *(TTP* 14.3)

If the "sole aim of Scripture" is to teach one to be moral, then Spinoza can claim biblical warrant for his distinction between external practice and internal belief. He continues: "The Bible teaches us itself, in numerous passages and with utter clarity, what each of us must do to obey God. It teaches that the entire Law consists in just one thing, namely love of one's neighbor" (*TTP* 14.3). The biblical message, the divine law, is a simple message of love and moral obedience. The Bible is essentially teaching us how to act, not what to believe. Spinoza arrives at this conclusion on the basis of his historical analysis of Scripture. However, in order to act in these appropriate ways, one must undergird those actions with certain minimal beliefs. These beliefs, which are necessary for the public practices commanded by Scripture, Spinoza defines as *faith*. He writes: "Faith can only be defined by, indeed can be nothing other than, acknowledging certain things about God, ignorance of which makes obedience towards him impossible and which are necessarily found wherever obedience is met with" (*TTP* 14.5). The *public faith*, which comprises those beliefs required for

THE UNIVERSAL RELIGION 95

acting justly and charitably, must be promoted by the state and publically endorsed by all citizens. This public faith is not the same thing as one's private religious opinions. One's individual opinions will, of course, extend much beyond the ("thin") public faith necessary for moral behavior. But for Spinoza, each individual in the state must share in the public faith, whatever else he also happens to believe. This public confession is not as ominous as it may appear. It should not be taken to be a form of brainwashing by the state. Every state necessarily promotes some minimal set of values and beliefs, and these values and beliefs need to be promulgated. Spinoza argues that the individual churches ought to be the primary vehicle in this regard.

Spinoza draws three important consequences from his definition of faith. First, he argues that "faith does not lead to salvation in itself, but only by means of obedience" (*TTP* 14.6). Faith without acts is not salvific. Simply holding certain beliefs does not particularly matter. What matters is actualizing them in appropriate ways. If one acts disobediently, unjustly, and uncharitably, then we may reasonably say of one that he does not share in the public confession. Second, Spinoza argues that "whoever is truly obedient [to the moral law] necessarily possesses the true faith which leads to salvation" (*TTP* 14.7). Obedience to the law is expressive of true faith, and truly salvific. By "salvation" Spinoza understands the *summum bonum*, the highest good and very best human life. "Faith," Spinoza continues,

> requires not so much truth as piety; and since faith is pious and apt for salvation only by way of obedience, no one is faithful except on the ground of obedience. It is, therefore, not the man who advances the best reasons who necessarily manifests the best faith but rather the man who performs the best works of justice and charity.

> (*TTP* 14.11)

Given Spinoza's definition of faith as the grounds for moral action – and nothing more – there is no need to test for private religious opinions to determine if one is "faithful". Observation of behavior is test enough. The Inquisition was an irrational

96 THE UNIVERSAL RELIGION

enterprise because it misunderstood the very concept of faith that it was seeking to instill in its victims.

The third major consequence of Spinoza's definition of faith is "that faith requires not so much true as pious dogmas, that is, such tenets as move the mind to obedience, even though many of these may not have a shadow of truth in them" (*TTP* 14.8). What matters when promulgating the public faith is whether the citizens are so moved by it that they actually commence to behave justly and charitably. This is the point of faith, after all. Any teaching, however grounded in superstition and dubious views, that actually gets people to behave morally is valuable. Spinoza writes:

> Intellectual knowledge of God, considering His nature as it is in itself, a nature which men cannot emulate by a certain rationale of living and cannot adopt as a paradigm for cultivating a true rationale of living, has no relevance whatsoever to faith and revealed religion, and consequently men may have totally the wrong ideas about God's nature without doing any wrong.
>
> (*TTP* 13.8)

Faith and pious action are not the possession of just those few who have achieved an "intellectual knowledge of God". On the contrary, Spinoza is keen to allow for a plurality of religious institutions, each of which is welcome to teach whatever and however it wishes, just so long as its parishioners come out on Sunday (or Saturday) more motivated to behave in morally and socially acceptable ways.

Acceptance of this diversity of pious dogmas is a necessity because of human nature. According to Spinoza, although human beings share a similarly rational nature, passions separate us as we seek different ways to deal with life's challenges (*E*4pp32–35). Such diversity is inevitable and must be accepted, and so we should accept a diversity of pious dogmas to be taught in the ideal republic. Spinoza writes that:

> People do not agree about everything; rather opinions govern men in different ways such that doctrines that move one person to devotion provoke another to derision and contempt. It follows that in the true

THE UNIVERSAL RELIGION 97

> universal and general faith pertain no dogmas capable of giving rise
> to controversy amongst honest people.
>
> (*TTP* 14.9)

The universal public faith must contain only those teachings and lessons that are needed for moral action. They must arouse no controversy, lest they bring back the very divisiveness they are meant to counter. In fact, the universal public faith seems to be a kind of minimal level of agreement that emerges from abstracting all idiosyncratic institutional considerations.

This separation of external religious practice with its accompanying universal public faith from the private opinions and pious dogmas of individual churches is a doctrine that seeks to draw a careful balance. It allows for enough agreement to gain a minimal consensus and thus, it is hoped, avoid anarchy and chaos, but enough diversity to avoid dictatorship. "How salutary and necessary," Spinoza exclaims, "this doctrine is in a society if we wish people to live in concord and peace with each other!" (*TTP* 14.11). By distinguishing public faith from private dogma, Spinoza hopes ultimately to advance stability and peace.

There are questions one might raise about Spinoza's recipe for civic harmony through public faith and good deeds. The distinction assumes a very strong dichotomy between public faith and private dogma. One may wonder whether public faith by itself has the requisite motivational thrust to bring about the kinds of action that harmonize disparate groups. Spinoza clearly looks to the churches and religious institutions to support in their own particular ways the public dogmas, but perhaps Spinoza could be a bit clearer about the importance of religious ritual in "materializing" the universal public message. The very formal, general nature of public faith is given an action-motivating boost from the pulpit, and the reader may wish that Spinoza outlined in greater detail precisely how this is supposed to work.

SPINOZA'S UNIVERSAL RELIGION OF CIVIC VIRTUE

Spinoza's Universal Religion is thus the set of beliefs necessary for good public behavior in an ideal republic. All citizens must

98 THE UNIVERSAL RELIGION

publically accept the dogmas of this faith – even radical atheists. To test the limits of Spinoza's public faith, we now examine in some detail the teachings of this Universal Religion. In our analysis we will pay special attention to the extreme case of Spinoza himself. Is Spinoza's Universal Religion expansive enough to include even radical atheists, like himself?

Spinoza's Universal Religion is constituted by seven dogmas that together share two important features:

(1) The dogmas are acceptable to all reasonable people of good will whatever their particular internal (private) religion.
(2) Believing the dogmas is necessary if one is to live a life of obedience, justice, and charity.

While everyone in the republic must publically endorse the dogmas of this religion, Spinoza claims that each of these dogmas can be "adapted" to individual beliefs (*TTP* 14.11). At a minimum, however, everyone in the republic must be able to at least state publically that she believes these seven teachings. The freedom to adapt these beliefs to one's private understandings is an important freedom. What matters is that each person adapts these claims to her own private understanding, and in so doing proceeds to *act* justly and charitably on the basis of that understanding (2 above). After examining each of the dogmas in turn and why it is deemed necessary for virtuous action, we then turn to the question of whether the dogma could be adapted to the Spinozistic system itself.

The first teaching of this public faith is that

> [1] There is a God (a supreme being), who is supremely just and merciful, or an exemplar of the true life, whom no one who does not know or who does not believe that He exists can obey or acknowledge as judge.

> (*TTP* 14.10)

The first dogma looks like a simple statement of belief in the God of the monotheistic religions. There exists a personal God who is morally good and so an "exemplar of the true life". This first teaching appears *prima facie* to rule out all forms of rationalistic deism, a belief in a non-personal God who created the world but does not interact with or care for it. Such a deistic God would not appear to be "just and merciful", since *ex hypothesi* he has no concern for his creation. Are deists to be excluded from civic life? Further, this dogma would seem to be problematic for Spinoza himself when we turn to his own metaphysical views. Certainly, Spinoza's one infinite substance is not "just and merciful". So can this dogma be "adapted" to Spinoza's own views?

First, Spinoza can surely assert in good conscience that he believes in (a) God, although in his case this refers to the one infinite substance of which every particular thing is a mode. So, on the most general level he can claim without disingenuousness to believe the key part of this first dogma, once it has been adapted to his own views. It seems to us that if both the theist and the non-theist can *meaningfully assert* that they "believe in [a] God", although what they will each mean by this is fundamentally different, then Spinoza's dogma provides some minimal common ground. Further, one may worry that Spinoza cannot seriously claim that his (impersonal) God is "supremely just and merciful, or an exemplar of the true life", but he may be able to accept even this claim on his own terms. For Spinoza, "knowledge of God is the mind's greatest good; and its greatest virtue is to know God" (*E*4p28). Further, he holds that the more one lives under the guidance of reason, the more one lives in harmony and agreement with one's fellows (*E*4pp35–37). In sum, Spinoza believes that true virtue and friendship follow from rational insight and knowledge of God, and given this, Spinoza may well conclude that God, a being infinitely rational, is "an exemplar of the true life", a model to emulate. Both the theist and the Spinozistic atheist seem to have reached at least nominal agreement here. This minimal level of agreement, a nominal consensus without (deep) philosophical agreement, seems to be at the heart of Spinoza's strategy in finding sufficient common ground to resolve disagreement without violence in a pluralistic world.

The second dogma of Spinoza's public faith is that:

> [2] He [God] is one; for no one can doubt that this too is absolutely required for supreme devotion, admiration and love towards God.

100 THE UNIVERSAL RELIGION

> Devotion, admiration and love, will arise only from the pre-eminence of one above all other things.

> (*TTP* 14.10)

This dogma about divine uniqueness allows each individual her own conception of God, so long as it is a being somehow supreme and exemplary. But however one conceives of God, this dogma indicates that divine pre-eminence grounds our devotion and love, both of God and of our fellows. From devotion to God springs devotion, commitment, even obedience to the State and its agenda of promoting peace and harmony. As with the first dogma and its suggestion that God is a moral exemplar, this one too draws a close connection between an understanding of divinity and the implications of this for political life.

To return to our test case, Spinoza would have no difficulty accepting this dogma, given his own metaphysical views and view of the *summum bonum*. As we have seen, the first dogma has already drawn a tight connection between knowledge of God and obedience to him, and this second dogma deepens the connection. The second dogma asserts that the very nature of divinity gives rise to "devotion, admiration and love", and this is consonant with Spinoza's own view, famously argued for in the second half of Part V of the *Ethics*. For Spinoza, love of God follows from knowledge of God, and the implications of this for moral and even political life are clear for Spinoza: living agreeably with one's fellows is a function of following the guidance of reason and the order of nature.

The third dogma of Spinoza's public faith is that:

> [3] He [God] is everywhere present and all things are manifest to Him; for if things were believed to be hidden from Him, or if it were not known that He sees all things, there would be doubts about the equity of His justice by which He directs all things, or it would even be unknown.

> (*TTP* 14.10)

Spinoza's third claim is that God (however one understands his nature) knows and directs everything. Spinoza believes this dogma is required for a moral life because a denial of it will call

THE UNIVERSAL RELIGION 101

into doubt God's goodness (the "equity of His justice"). We need to believe that God is omnipresent, everywhere directing an ordered world (somehow), in order to assure ourselves that the world is ultimately a just place. Taking the first three dogmas together, we should note the close connection between God's nature and the role God plays in the promotion of justice, mercy, love, and equity through the medium of a universal religion. Spinoza's overarching goal here is to clarify the very important role that religion plays in the communal life of the State. In this case too, we do not believe that Spinoza would have much difficulty adapting this dogma to his own views. Spinoza argues in the *Ethics* that one of the attributes of the one substance (God) is Thought (*E*2p1). The one substance includes ideas of all of the things that exist (*E*2p3), and in its own way, Spinoza's God is omniscient. Spinoza can in good conscience endorse this claim about divine omniscience and providence.

The fourth dogma of Spinoza's public faith is that

> [4] He [God] possesses supreme right and dominion over all things; nor is anything that He does compelled by laws, but He does all things at His absolute pleasure and by His unique grace. For all men are obliged to obey Him absolutely but He is obliged to obey no one.
>
> (*TTP* 14.10)

This dogma asserts that God is subject to nothing but his own nature. He is omnipotent, while human beings are not. Human beings are dependent beings, and the importance of this dogma is that such dependent beings need to be instructed in unfettered loyalty to God. In preaching obedience to God, the civic religion (through the medium of the individual churches) preaches obedience to authority. Here, too, Spinoza could adapt this dogma to his own philosophical views, for he believes that everything is part of God, and we must in some way assimilate our being to that greater whole of which we are but a part. Spinoza claims in the *Ethics* that God is constrained by nothing and so is absolutely free (*E*1d7, *E*1p35). By contrast we are dependent beings, and become (relatively) free by aligning our being with God, that is, by acting from our own rational nature.

102 THE UNIVERSAL RELIGION

The fifth dogma of Spinoza's public faith provides the rationale for the previous four:

> [5] Worship of God and obedience to Him consist solely in justice and charity, or in love of one's neighbor.
>
> (*TTP* 14.10)

Having established in the first four propositions of his public faith that we should be totally devoted to the one God, who is absolutely supreme, knows and directs everything, and is limited by nothing, Spinoza then argues that this devotion consists solely in public acts of justice and charity. Spinoza here makes a transition to the more practical, political realm, by clarifying the practical intent of the earlier dogmas. As clear as this dogma is, it is in fact more problematic than the earlier ones. The first four pronouncements about God's existence, uniqueness, omniscience, and omnipotence are immediately acceptable by any theist, and as we have seen by Spinoza himself. However, the claim that worship of God consists *only* in acts of justice and charity is far more controversial. What about specific ritual practices, which all religions enjoin for the correct worship of God? This "practical" dogma, which defines worship *"solely"* as acts of loving-kindness, seems hard to square with the beliefs and practices of the traditional religions. But, for Spinoza, this claim is central because it is just the diverse private, and sectarian professions and ritual practices that cause the unhealthy and destabilizing divisions in society. This fifth dogma is his attempt to ensure that in addition to whatever differences and idiosyncrasies attach themselves to particular religions, there needs to be a commitment *above all* to love of neighbor, to justice, charity, and tolerance. The Golden Rule resonates in both Judaism and Christianity, and Spinoza's invocation of it as the rationale for public belief in God is rhetorically very powerful. But we should not lose sight of the political role of the dogma here. It is quite explicitly the means to bring about civic stability and harmony.

Though it is *prima facie* at odds with traditional belief and practice, perhaps both the Church and Spinoza could find common ground and accept this dogma. Perhaps the Church could come to understand "worship" as "public worship" and good deeds, while understanding more idiosyncratic kinds of worship and practice (e.g., the Eucharist) as obligatory with respect to one's private life and spiritual development. Likewise, we do not believe that Spinoza would have much difficulty adapting this dogma to his own system, given his claims in Part IV of the *Ethics* that the rational man, precisely on account of his knowledge (worship) of God, behaves in just and charitable ways (*E*4pp35–37). In this way, this controversial dogma may prove acceptable across the aisle.

The sixth dogma is a support to the fifth:

> [6] All who obey God in this rationale of living, and only these, are saved; those who live under the sway of pleasures are lost. If people did not firmly believe this, there would be no reason why they should obey God rather than their own pleasures.
>
> (*TTP* 14.10)

Given that there is only one God to whom we must be completely devoted, and given that the worship of this one God consists solely in acting justly and charitably, Spinoza adds that those who do act justly and charitably will be rewarded by God ("saved"). No single idea of the precise nature of "salvation" is defined, of course. Each person may understand salvation as he wishes, including of course Spinoza himself. The important point is that each individual believes that something good will result if one is just and charitable and, contrarily, something bad will happen if one is not. Virtue may be its own reward, or not. In any event, the crucial point is that this dogma gives one a strong incentive to worship the one God through moral action. It is important, Spinoza thinks, for this dogma to arouse strong emotions and motivations to act appropriately. Spinoza argues in the *Ethics* that the only way to combat a strong emotion is with another powerful and contrary emotion (*E*4p7). We are constantly tempted to act in ways that are not just and charitable. Thus, we need some powerful contrary emotion to combat these temptations – the fear of hell and the desire for heaven is just such a powerful emotion. As one becomes more intellectually and emotionally mature, the need for such strong emotions will diminish because one will instead desire to act morally from more dispassionate reasons.

104 THE UNIVERSAL RELIGION

Spinoza would not have too much trouble adapting this dogma in such a way that he could assent to it. He argues in the *Ethics* that by acting virtuously one achieves the highest good that is possible for human beings. Famously, the very last proposition (*E*5p42) claims to prove that one acts virtuously not for some reward, but because virtue itself is the reward. Spinoza could well understand salvation ("one goes to heaven by worshiping God") as "one lives the best kind of life by living morally". This dogma has sufficient flexibility to accommodate Spinoza and other atheists.

The seventh and last dogma deals with a potential problem, and reads:

> [7] Finally, God forgives the repentant their sins; for there is no one who does not sin, and therefore if this were not clearly established, all would despair of their salvation and would have no reason to believe that God is merciful. But anyone who firmly believes that God forgives men's sins with the mercy and grace with which He directs all things and is more fully inspired with the love of God for this reason, truly knows Christ according to the spirit, and Christ is within him.
>
> (*TTP* 14.10)

We are not always just and charitable, and thus if the public faith demanded perfection of us, then none of us could live up to it. Despair would replace active engagement, and a disengagement from political life would follow. The public faith must make room for improvement. We must be able to recognize when we and others have behaved immorally and learn to forgive. In so doing we manifest love for God and neighbor, and here we may see connections to earlier dogmas. While it is true that Spinoza's metaphysical determinism and doctrine of virtue make no room for repentance and forgiveness (*E*4p54), he could adapt this dogma to his system in something like the following way: Even though metaphysical determinism is true, and hence repentance and forgiveness are pointless, this does not entail that the future must be like the past. Who knows what the future will bring? (This is known only to God.) As a result, past immoral action may give way to moral improvement. This antidote to despair or inaction is Spinozistic and consistent with the general intent of the last dogma.

THE UNIVERSAL RELIGION 105

In invoking Christ in this last dogma, we may note in general, and not surprisingly, that Spinoza's discussion of religion and religious dogma is presented at the level of popular imagination. Such a presentation is a sign of his "realism", of a measured sense of what has a chance of acceptance and success in the social and political world in which he lived. In this last dogma about repentance and forgiveness, we are reminded of Spinoza's commitment to what we have called "weak normativity", a predilection for prescription without underlying censure. Spinoza recommends beneficial actions, but does not blame or censure those who fail to so act. In general, Spinoza's revisionist conception of religion and the Universal Religion are designed to aid the various existing religious communities within a given state to educate their parishioners to act in these beneficial ways. As we have seen, there is conceptual room in his account for the (non-theistic) philosopher and his "worship", even though such worship is a non-starter for everyone else. Given this diversity, Spinoza is right to appeal so strongly to the imagination and the emotions. For Spinoza, the goal is to get the religious communities and their leaders to promote from the pulpit harmony and peace.

CONCLUSION

While Spinoza does not seek uniformity of religious opinion in his ideal republic, he is strongly committed to finding common ground among the citizenry. The dogmas of the Universal Religion are meant to ensure this. The Universal Religion contains three parts: first, a belief in a supreme being to whom one is more devoted to than to anything else (dogmas 1–4); second, a belief that true worship of this supreme being and personal salvation itself is brought about (only) by acting justly and charitably (dogmas 5–6); third, a belief that when one falls short, one can make amends and start again to try to act justly and charitably (dogma 7). In short, the dogmas command love of God, of neighbor, and of self. As long as one's religious belief system and outlook presuppose these, one will be in step with the public faith and the common good. Spinoza has a keen sense of what he can reasonably hope for in the political setting of his time. Churches (and traditional religion) are not going to disappear, and Spinoza well understands that the State must work with and through them to bring about the political changes that he believes are necessary for political stability. Spinoza does not have a very optimistic view of human beings and their capacities to live without superstition, and as a result the dogmas of the Universal Religion are presented in such a way that they will be readily understood by all citizens. In addition, Spinoza carves out a place in the (modern) state for non-theists or atheists, like himself. Spinozistic atheism can be accommodated to the public faith, as we have seen. As we move on to discuss in our final two chapters toleration and democracy, it will be important to keep in mind this basic structure of belief and commitment to love of God, neighbor, and self that everyone shares in the ideal republican commonwealth. We will come to see that what really is being inculcated are not dogmas about what to believe and how to act, but rather a set of virtues, precisely the "liberal" virtues necessary for a vibrant, working democratic state. Cultivation of these virtues and acting in accordance with them ensures, Spinoza believes, sufficient consensus to make a peaceful resolution of conflicts possible without agreement on fundamental questions.

FURTHER READING

On Spinoza's Universal Religion, see Rosenthal (2001a). For some historical context and analysis, see Nadler (2011, chapters 7–8) and James (2012, chapters 8–9). On why Spinoza cannot call for the abolition of religion, see De Dijn (2013), and for the relationship between religion and politics in Spinoza's theory, see Halper (2004).

6

TOLERATION

INTRODUCTION

The seventeenth century saw many tracts on toleration, with Locke's *Letter Concerning Toleration* (1689) being the most celebrated. Spinoza's theory of toleration predates Locke's and is more expansive, covering not only freedom of religious practice, but also freedom of thought and speech, including that of non-believers. Spinoza's theory of toleration also has an important role to play in the whole of his democratic theory, as we shall see in the next chapter. For Spinoza, toleration is not defended for its own sake, however, and is not grounded in any sort of liberal theory of individual rights. Toleration, Spinoza tells us, is a necessary condition for political stability, peace, and individual virtue. The subtitle of the *Theological-Political Treatise* states that the goal of the book is to "demonstrate that freedom to philosophize may not only be allowed without danger to piety and the stability of the republic but cannot be refused without destroying the peace of the republic and piety itself". In this chapter we examine Spinoza's argument for this conclusion.

108 TOLERATION

Let us begin with a definition. By *toleration* we understand "an allowing or forbearing what is disapproved and may be prevented" (Raphael 1988). Over the course of the next two chapters we will see that Spinoza moves freely between two different conceptions of toleration. The first is the legal toleration of certain activities as the result of policy decisions taken by the sovereign. The second is the virtue of toleration as inculcated by social institutions and beneficial for social stability and harmony. The two are, of course, intimately related to one another.

Spinoza's argument for toleration proceeds in three steps. First, he argues for subjecting all religious authority to political authority. These arguments at first seem strange because they seem to give *unlimited* authority to the sovereign in religious matters. But they are, in fact, necessary for the arguments that follow. In making these arguments Spinoza is rejecting the "two swords" view inherent in the Christendom Model, a view committed to reciprocal power sharing between Church and State. These arguments are significant because they require an entirely new paradigm for thinking about the relationship between the Church and the State.

Second, after arguing that all religious authority is subject to the sovereign, Spinoza then argues for an expansive freedom of speech and conscience. As we shall see, Spinoza's arguments for freedom of speech here are, however, more complex and conflicted than is often recognized. Spinoza does not grant an unlimited freedom of speech and the freedom that he does defend is more restrictive than contemporary American constitutional law grants. Nevertheless, Spinoza defends by far the most expansive freedom of speech and conscience of any early modern thinker.

The third step in Spinoza's argument is to argue that toleration and liberty of thought and conscience are necessary for individual virtue and freedom, and as a result for political stability. A free state (a liberal republic) does not depend on the kind of homogeneity that the Christendom Model advocated. The only common ground that is required for political stability and human fulfillment is that generated out of a commitment to the dogmas of the Universal Religion, which we examined in the last chapter. As we have seen, the Universal Religion supports justice, charity, and neighborliness, and these virtues provide the foundation for toleration.

By contrast, Spinoza argues that the sectarian exclusivism inherent in the Christendom Model breeds intolerance, bigotry, and hysteria. Such citizens create a less, not a more, stable society. Toleration for diversity of opinion is thus a necessary, but not a sufficient, condition for the creation of virtuous citizens. We end this chapter with a brief comparison of Spinoza's views on toleration with the more famous views of Locke. This comparison helps to bring into sharper relief the unique aspects of Spinoza's view.

RELIGIOUS AUTHORITY IS SUBORDINATE TO POLITICAL POWER

According to Spinoza, there can only be one source of authority in the state and that source is the sovereign. In arguing for the subjugation of religious authority to secular authority Spinoza is perhaps frankly acknowledging a trend that was already taking place: "Whether we take the Church of England, the Lutheran Churches in Germany and Scandinavia, or the Catholic Church in the Habsburg or Bourdon dominions," one historian writes, "the picture is basically the same: a tight union of the Church and State, with the Church reduced to the junior partner" (Bokenkotter 2004: 274). This (Erastian) subordination of the authority of the Church to the authority of the State may be seen as a liberalizing, autonomy-enhancing move away from the Christendom Model of society and toward a modern, democratic conception of political life. The effect of this transition was to limit religious authority over individuals and thereby to create a *civil* community. In the new order a religious authority held power only over those who elected to join a particular religious organization. By contrast, the sovereign had immediate and "involuntary" control over all who inhabited a particular territory.

Spinoza argues that when religious authorities claim a divine right that allows them to make laws that contradict the sovereign's laws "no one can fail to see that all this is utterly destructive of the common good of the republic" (*TTP* 20.16). Following the Wars of Religion and the fragile peace instituted by the Peace of Westphalia, it was not difficult to see the need to reduce the political power of confessional religious faiths. Spinoza's arguments for this

110 TOLERATION

conclusion, however, are not historical. Rather Spinoza gives four philosophical arguments for his conclusion. We term these arguments: the State of Nature Argument, the Force of Law Argument, the Definition Argument, and the Sovereign Authority Argument. In this section we examine these four arguments, formalize them to reveal their logical structure, and briefly examine them. Interestingly, not all of these arguments lead to the conclusion that the sovereign's authority is limited only to actions. Some of these arguments by themselves entail much greater sovereign authority over the religious lives of the populace.

The first argument is the State of Nature Argument. Spinoza writes:

> Everyone [in the state of nature] therefore is obliged to live solely by their own decisions and not by someone else's, and they are not bound to acknowledge anyone as judge or as the rightful defender of religion. I affirm that the sovereign has retained this right. While he may consult advisors, he is not obliged to recognize anyone as judge or any mortal except himself as defender of any right, other than a prophet expressly sent by God who has proved this by incontrovertible signs. Even then it is not a man whom he is compelled to recognize but rather God himself. Should the sovereign refuse to obey God in his revealed law, he may do so, but at his own peril and to his own loss. No civil or natural law forbids him.
>
> (*TTP* 16.20)

As we reconstruct this argument, it is something like the following:

(1) In a state of nature no one has a natural authority over another in matters of religion. (Premise 1)
(2) The sovereign remains in a state of nature even after civil society has come into existence. (Premise 2)
(3) Therefore, no one has natural authority over the sovereign in matters of religion. (From 1, 2)

This argument is similar to ones given by Hobbes in *Leviathan* (2.26.2). One of the fundamental ideas in Hobbes' argument is that citizens in a civil society remain in a state of nature, without legal protection, relative to the sovereign, who is not party to the social contract that created the society. The transfer of rights to the sovereign, who is the ultimate authority and judge in any dispute, creates a power imbalance and this grants the sovereign absolute authority. Does Spinoza accept this claim as well? Spinoza suggests this idea when he writes that "no offense can be committed against subjects by sovereigns, since they [the sovereigns] are of right permitted to all things, and therefore offenses occur only between private persons obliged by law not to harm one another" (*TTP* 16.14). The sovereign cannot do a wrong to a citizen because the sovereign determines what counts as a wrong. It seems that on Spinoza's view sovereigns must remain in something like a state of nature relative to their citizens and vice versa, just as Hobbes suggests.

These claims appear to give the sovereign unlimited authority over the religious lives of the citizens. This smacks of totalitarianism, not a promising start for one committed to religious freedom. *Prima facie* Spinoza's argument here seems far too strong. He has concluded that religious authorities cannot give commands to the sovereign, which is the conclusion that he wants because the sovereign's authority in religious matters is supreme. But such a claim then seems to entail that the sovereigns themselves do not need to respect the citizen's beliefs on private religious matters, which is a conclusion that Spinoza does not want. This argument appears to grant to the sovereign the right to dictate private religious preferences to the citizenry.

This political authority is, however, not as unlimited as it at first appears to be. The sovereign's authority in religious matters is limited in two different ways. First, the sovereign's authority in religious matters is limited only to *actions*. Second, Spinoza explicitly argues that a prophet who has proved by signs that he has been sent forth by God would have authority over the sovereign. Given Spinoza's views about prophecy, this is a strange concession and it is not entirely clear why he is making it. In any event, as Spinoza says, no civil or natural law requires the sovereign to obey the prophetic messenger. So what might the reason be for the authority of the prophet? Perhaps Spinoza has something like the following in mind: In commanding great respect among the

112 TOLERATION

masses the prophet would perforce have real political power, and such power would limit the sovereign's authority. The sovereign is thus best advised to take seriously this divine messenger. The real point is that the only issue is one of power and the possible limits to authority that results from it.

The second argument for the reduction of the political power of religious authority in the state we call the Force of Law Argument. This argument is given in the following passage where Spinoza writes:

> Justice therefore and all the doctrines of true reason without exception, including charity toward our neighbor, receive the force of law and command from the authority of the state alone, that is ... solely from the decree of those who have the right to rule. Now because, as I have already shown, the kingdom of God consists solely in the law of justice, charity, and true religion, it follows that God has no kingdom over men except through those who hold power.
>
> (*TTP* 19.5)

We have earlier argued that there are only two kinds of law for Spinoza: laws of nature, which describe how things behave in the universe, and human laws, including civil laws created by the sovereign political authority (*TTP* 4.1). There are no natural moral laws that apply solely to humans and that humans are blameworthy for not following. Given this assumption, this argument can be reconstructed as follows:

(1) There is no obligation to obey any law and "doctrines of true reason" (justice and charity) unless following these laws and doctrines also *seems* to be in our own best interest. (Premise 1)

(2) Whenever the sovereign commands that all obey some law and underwrites this command with a credible threat of force, this action by the sovereign causes the law to *seem* to all citizens as though obeying it is in their own best interest. (Premise 2)

(3) So only after a sovereign commands that all obey a rule of reason is a citizen certainly under an obligation to do so. (From 1, 2)

TOLERATION 113

(4) Therefore, rational (and religious) rules for conduct do not obligate all citizens until, and for only so long as, the sovereign commands these laws and backs them up with a credible threat of force. (From 3)

What is interesting here is that the rules of justice and the principle of charity (love of neighbor) do not possess any inherent binding authority. For Spinoza, there are no moral laws that obligate unconditionally. Only when the rational rules of conduct are underwritten and enforced by sanctions do they gain the power to compel. As Spinoza says, "God has no special kingship over men except through those who exercise government" (*TTP* 19.3). There is no higher authority than the sovereign. Even justice and charity fall under his sway.

This argument appears to make assumptions similar to the assumptions made by certain schools of Legal Positivism. According to Austin, for example, a law is a command given to a group of people by a sovereign and backed up by a credible threat of force (Austin 1995 [1832], Lecture V). Civil laws on this view have no essential connection to morality. All that is required for an edict to be a law is that it be commanded to a populace and backed up by a credible threat of force. Such Positivism was hardly the norm in Spinoza's (and Hobbes') time. In the seventeenth century almost all legal theorists were Natural Law theorists. They argued that there is some kind of essential connection between law, morality, and reason. Irrational or immoral laws on this view are not laws at all. The classic defense for this view was made by Aquinas in the thirteenth century (*Summa Theologiae* I–II, qq. 90–97).

Is Spinoza defending a form of legal positivism similar to Austin's later influential theory? He certainly seems to be. Spinoza's position here, like Austin's, entails the conclusion that civil laws can be promulgated regardless of their rationality or morality, and if the sovereign unwisely commands laws that undermine the strength of the republic, then the state will collapse, not because the laws are immoral but simply because they are ineffective.

Nevertheless, Spinoza's position is somewhat different from that of the later Legal Positivists. While Spinoza does believe that there can be irrational and immoral laws (*PT* 3.6), and that

114 TOLERATION

morality and law can conflict, the impetus for his view and the conclusions he reaches are at key points at odds with the later Legal Positivists like Austin and Hart. Spinoza's political concerns are quite different from the Positivists and his understanding of morality is radically different. In defining the relationship between civil law and religion, and in subordinating the latter to the former, Spinoza is led to a certain rapprochement between law and morality. In this context, by "morality" we intend those laws and virtues that tend toward social stability and positive freedom. As we have seen, Spinoza totally rejects any form of independent normative moral law that binds only on humans. For his part, Spinoza is concerned with the law's role as a teacher of virtue. Cultivating individual virtue then provides the grounds for political stability and freedom. As a result, while law and morality are distinct, they are implicated in one another. In commanding justice and charity the sovereign is at once promulgating law *and* engaging in social engineering. The sovereign at once holds political power *and* by means of the law teaches virtue. (Moses is paradigmatic for Spinoza here, see *TTP* 5.10–11, 19.21.) Spinoza is not concerned, as the Legal Positivists are, with carving out a sacred space for a private morality, which is immune from legal sanction. Rather, he argues for a sovereign authority that is at once powerful *and* wise, who secures stability not only through fear and legal sanction, but also by inculcating virtue in the citizenry. The Universal Religion is the baseline, and its promulgation is an attempt to secure stability in the state by means of inculcating certain virtues. This is not part of the Legal Positivist agenda. In reacting to the Natural Law tradition, the Legal Positivist emphasizes a commitment to individual rights and private morality that is not part of Spinoza's concern. As we shall see in the next chapter, Spinoza's "liberalism" is not a commitment to libertarian ("negative") freedom.

In sum, for Spinoza, the political sovereign, not the religious authority, makes the law and this promulgation makes certain actions right (legal) and others wrong (illegal). No appeal seems possible, and the individual must obey the sovereign's laws or commands, whatever they are (*PT* 3.6). But the sovereign is ultimately concerned with more than just obedience. As Spinoza famously declares at the end of the *TTP:*

> It is not the purpose of the state to turn people from rational beings into beasts or automata, but rather to allow their minds and bodies to develop in their own ways in security and enjoy the free use of reason ... Therefore, the true purpose of the state is in fact freedom.
>
> (*TTP* 20.6)

The third argument for the subordination of religious authority to state power similarly rests on the claim that civil law and religion cannot really come into conflict. We call this argument the Definition Argument and Spinoza hints at it in his discussion of the first argument. Spinoza writes:

> From this, it emerges very evidently in what sense the sovereign authorities are interpreters of religion; we also understand that no one can rightly obey God, if they do not adapt pious observance to which everyone is bound, to the public interest, and if, as a consequence, they do not obey all the decrees of the sovereign power. For we are obliged by God's decree to treat with piety all persons without exception and inflict harm on no one ... But no private person can know what is in the interest of the state other than from the decrees of the sovereign authorities, who alone have the responsibility to transact public business.
>
> (*TTP* 19.11)

We reconstruct this argument in the following way:

(1) Obeying God demands pious observance. (Premise 1)
(2) Pious observance requires (at least in part) acting in the public good and doing harm to no one. (Premise 2)
(3) The sovereign defines what is in the *public good* and what counts as a *harm* (as opposed to a simple *injury*) to another citizen. (Premise 3)
(4) Therefore, the sovereign defines (at least in part) what pious observance consists in. (From 1–3)
(5) Therefore, religious authorities cannot act or teach against the laws or rulings of the sovereign without disobeying God. (From 4)

116 TOLERATION

If this argument is correct, then it appears in principle impossible for religious authorities to claim that their sphere of influence has been invaded by the sovereign. The religious authorities cannot argue that the civil laws violate the requirements of their religion. Religion requires of us "pious observance ... to the public interest", a claim entailing a general law-abidingness and obedience. But it is the sovereign who defines the laws, and without the sovereign, the religious imperative is vacuous. On any occasion when a religious authority calls into question the laws of the sovereign, such an authority would be preaching impiety and so would, in effect, be violating her own religious obligations. In this way, religious authority is subject to political authority.

The rhetoric of Spinoza's claim here is interesting. In intertwining piety with legal conformity, Spinoza hopes to break down the historical dichotomy between religious obligations and other non-religious ones. If he can convince us that obedience to the state is a form of piety, he has gone a long way to providing compelling reason to understand and accept the supreme authority of the state over religion. No longer can the Church demand obedience on grounds other than the public interest, and with this the authority of the Church is significantly curbed.

The last argument that Spinoza gives for the subordination of religious authority to political power we call the Sovereign Authority Argument. Spinoza argues that sovereigns

> can assuredly make no decision whatever about war or peace or anything else, if they are obliged to wait upon the opinion of another person to tell them whether the policy they judge to be in the interests of the state is pious or impious. On the contrary, everything will depend upon the decision of the one who possesses the right to judge and decree what is pious and what is impious, what is holy and what is sacrilegious.
>
> *(TTP* 19.16)

The central idea in this passage is that a sovereign authority cannot be both *sovereign* and require the approval of religious authorities to act. To be sovereign he must have control over

TOLERATION **117**

religion and not the other way around. More formally, we reconstruct the argument as follows:

(1) A sovereign authority is the final authority on questions of state and has absolute and un-checkable power to decide questions of state (such as war and peace, the laws of the republic, taxation policy). (Premise 1)
(2) If religious authorities could veto or constrain the decisions of the sovereign, then the sovereign no longer has sovereign authority. (From 1)
(3) A sovereign must have sovereign authority to be a sovereign. (Premise 2)
(4) Thus, the sovereign cannot be bound by religious rules or authorities. (From 2, 3)

This argument appears to be grounded in Spinoza's claims concerning right and power, which we examined in chapter two. In that chapter we examined Spinoza's claim that a sovereign has the right to do whatever is in his power to do. If that is correct, then for a sovereign to have the right to decide questions of state, he must possess the power to do so. But he only has the absolute power to do so if his decision cannot be checked by religious authorities. Thus, it seems as though Spinoza must conclude that to be a genuine sovereign – that is, someone who can ultimately decide questions of state – one must have *sovereign authority* or an absolute and un-checkable authority. And this authority means that one is not subject to the approval of any religious authority.

If this is the correct way to reconstruct Spinoza's reasoning here, then he seems to reject any notion of a "checks and balances" system of power as argued for by Montesquieu, Locke, and the American Founders, though it should be noted that Spinoza has, unsurprisingly, a very keen sense of the possible abuse of power by the sovereign authority (*PT* 7.1). A "checks and balances" approach to sovereign power is one in which the sovereign authority has been diffused among different powers who each have the ability to veto or modify the decisions of the others. Some authors, such as Hobbes, famously argued that such a system is logically incoherent because there must always be some power that in the end has

118 TOLERATION

final and un-checkable sovereign authority (*Leviathan* 2.18.16). Someone, the argument goes, must have the final word and that person is the sovereign authority. The authors of the American Constitution rejected these arguments and created a system with a diffuse and complex power structure. In this debate Spinoza seems to side clearly with Hobbes and Bodin and against Montesquieu and Locke. Those who argued – and many did – that religious institutions serve as a means of checking the sovereign's power must be mistaken. Spinoza seems to think that such a check on the sovereign's power is not needed. He writes:

> It is indeed certain that if those who exercise power aspire to go their own way [i.e., following the passions rather than reason], whether they possess authority in sacred matters or not, everything, both sacred and secular, will rapidly deteriorate, and all the faster if private men make a seditious attempt themselves to champion divine right. Therefore, absolutely nothing is achieved by denying this right to sovereigns.
>
> (*TTP* 19.19)

The argument here seems to be that if the sovereign institutes bad laws (laws that are ineffective and do not lead to the health of the state), then things will deteriorate and eventually fall apart. That is so whether or not there is some power external to the sovereign that attempts to stop the sovereign from so acting. Spinoza's curious argument here is that things will more quickly deteriorate if "private men make a seditious attempt themselves to champion divine right" (*TTP* 19.19). Political dissolution will occur more quickly if religious authorities attempt to check or control the power of the sovereign by invoking religious claims. Why is that? It is because these authorities will end up instituting an alternative political power structure that will have to claim for itself sovereign authority, at least in some matters. In order to challenge the sovereign authority, religious authorities will have to claim this authority for themselves. There are two problems with religious authorities claiming sovereign authority over the existing sovereign. First, in such a state with two sovereign entities the state is already divided against itself. Such a society that is already divided against itself in this way can really be thought of as two different states existing in the same geographical location, rather than as a single harmonious one. Second, Spinoza believes that religious authorities are likely to be more prejudiced and passionate when compared to secular political authorities. Thus, they are much less likely to create rational and effective laws, and so it is more likely that "everything, both sacred and secular, will rapidly deteriorate," even faster than under an ineffective sovereign (*TTP* 19.19).

In short, Spinoza argues that religious authority must be subject to political power because (i) the sovereign remains in a state of nature relative to the populace (including religious authorities), (ii) the laws of reason and religion have no obligatory force until the sovereign commands them, (iii) the sovereign defines the public good and religion enjoins promotion of this public good, and finally because (iv) the sovereign needs absolute sovereign authority to rule. These four arguments together give the sovereign enormous control over religious institutions. This leads immediately to the worry of what is to be done if the sovereign dictates what many in the state believe to be irreligious. What if the sovereign authority commands the population to worship him as divine? Wouldn't it be reasonable for the disaffected to resist this command of the sovereign? To address this issue we must examine other arguments that Spinoza gives concerning the *limits* of sovereign power.

SOVEREIGN POWER HAS NATURAL LIMITS

The power of the sovereign over individuals has natural limits. The sovereign's power can concern itself only with how people *act* and not with what people *believe* or even, with some qualifications, *say*. "No one," Spinoza writes, "will ever be able to transfer his power and (consequently) his right to another person in such a way that he ceases to be a human being; and there will never be a sovereign power that can dispose of everything just as it pleases" (*TTP* 17.1). Rather, when entering civil society each individual "surrendered his right to act according to his own resolution, but not his right to think and judge for himself" (*TTP* 20.7). Given that the right of the sovereign is coextensive with his natural power, it follows that

120 TOLERATION

the sovereign does not have the right to do something that he cannot do. And one thing that a sovereign cannot do is to command someone to hold certain beliefs. Spinoza argues that decrees

> designed to regulate religion which were intended to put an end to [theological] disputes, actually have quite the opposite effect, stirring people up rather than disciplining them while other men deem themselves authorized by such laws to arrogate a boundless license to themselves.

> (*TTP* 20.15)

This claim gives Spinoza an argument for an expansive freedom of conscience on religious and philosophical questions. Spinoza's freedom of conscience includes both the right to believe whatever one wishes to believe and the right to say publicly what one believes. This liberty of expression will extend to include atheists and all who subscribe (at least nominally) to the dogmas of the Universal Religion, previously outlined. This liberty is far more expansive than that offered by any other early modern thinker. Locke's toleration doctrine, for example, explicitly excludes atheists because "Promises, Covenants, and Oaths, which are the Bonds of Human Society, can have no hold upon an Atheist" (Locke 1983 [1689]: 51).

Although it is an expansive liberty, Spinoza's understanding of freedom of conscience is not exactly ours. Spinoza writes that "no one can *act* against the sovereign's decisions without prejudicing his [the sovereign's] authority, but they can *think and judge* and consequently *also speak* without any restriction" (*TTP* 20.7; italics added). It appears that Spinoza is granting broad freedom of expression that will allow individuals to say whatever they think on religious and political questions. But then he adds: "provided they merely speak or teach by way of reason alone, not by trickery or in anger or from hatred or with the intention of introducing some alteration in the state on their own initiative" (*TTP* 20.7). The right to speak one's mind is not an unlimited right. Spinoza argues that every citizen has by nature a freedom of conscience that cannot be alienated, but then he asserts that this freedom is limited to *rational arguments* about religious and political questions. If one cannot discourse about religion or politics "by way of reason

TOLERATION **121**

alone", then one abrogates the right to speak about what one believes. Spinoza does not grant a universal, unconditional right to say whatever you happen to think, but only a right to argue rationally about what you believe. Spinoza explains his restriction here with a helpful example. He asks us to

> suppose someone shows a law to be contrary to sound reason and voices the opinion that it should be repealed. If at the same time they submit their view to the sovereign power and in the meantime do nothing contrary to what the law commands, they surely deserve well of their country, as every good citizen does.
>
> (*TTP* 20.7)

For Spinoza, citizens are allowed to object to the laws of the sovereign so long as they do so in an orderly way and obey the law while objecting to it. Perhaps even civil disobedience is allowable, though this is far from clear. Spinoza suggests that if the rational arguments are strong enough and presented clearly, and that the proponent of the argument behaves in a civil way, then a responsible sovereign has good reason to give it a hearing. It is important to keep in mind that the sovereign is empowered to stabilize the state by instruction. He is not a Hobbesian strongman who brooks no opposition. This is in large part why Spinoza favors democracy, and we will return to this issue in the next chapter. Such openness may seem utopian, but it is good to remember that Spinoza believes that bad, ineffective laws will surely lead to the collapse of the state. So it really is in the sovereign's best interest to listen to all citizens of good will. We may thus expect that the laws of the state will become progressively more effective (more "rational") over time as more arguments are considered. All depends, however, on good will and a desire to be helpful to the state and its goals. Citizens may not use their freedom to slander the sovereign or make "a seditious attempt to abolish the law against the magistrate's will" (*TTP* 20.7). Only the sovereign can abolish a law, so even if the law is in fact counterproductive, and irrational in this sense, we must obey it while we attempt convince the sovereign that the law should be repealed (*TTP* 16.8).

122 TOLERATION

Spinoza's views on freedom of conscience are also complicated by his insistence that there are actually some views that cannot ever be advocated in a civil society. Spinoza argues that the mere proclamation of some views is dangerous. There are some beliefs "which, simply by being put forward, dissolve the agreement by which each person surrenders their right to act according to their own judgment" (*TTP* 20.9). For examples of such inherently dangerous views Spinoza argues that "it is seditious for anyone to hold that a sovereign power does not have an autonomous right or that one should not keep a promise or that everyone should live according to their own judgment" (*TTP* 20.9). These views are so harmful that even stating them should be outlawed. Spinoza writes that by "the very fact that someone thinks such a thing, they are tacitly or explicitly breaking the pact that they made with the sovereign" (*TTP* 20.9). Advocating such views undercuts the conditions necessary for a peaceful and harmonious state, and hence are to be outlawed. Those beliefs that are necessary for the very possibility of a civil society cannot be challenged within that society. By participating in the communal life of civil society one must accept the conditions necessary for its existence. This is the point often brought forth by religious thinkers in Spinoza's time who, under the sway of the Christendom Model, argued that certain religious beliefs were vitally necessary for the existence of a peaceful society. These beliefs were then beyond question within that society. Spinoza accepts the same basic principle, in holding that certain foundational issues are beyond discussion, but he substitutes non-sectarian beliefs stemming from his Universal Religion for the sectarian beliefs put forth by Church authorities. In sum, by not founding the state on sectarian religion, Spinoza is able to exclude sectarian religious beliefs from that quarantined set of beliefs that are beyond discussion. Rousseau held precisely the same view in the *Social Contract* (4.8), and the one negative dogma of his own civil religion, "No intolerance", would be readily accepted by Spinoza. Both Spinoza and Rousseau are intolerant of intolerance in order to maintain political stability.

It may be helpful to note in passing how different Spinoza's views on freedom of speech are from contemporary American views. In American constitutional law, as it has developed in the

TOLERATION **123**

twentieth century, certain areas of speech have been rendered illegal, specifically such speech that presents a "clear and present danger" or, as later clarified by the court, such speech that both advocates immediate lawless action and is likely to produce that action (*Schenck v. United States* [1919]). American law also places such speech that involves "fighting words" outside the bounds of what is legally allowable, but has been consistently shrinking the number of actual words banned (*Chaplinsky v. New Hampshire* [1942]). The State is almost never allowed to ban speech on the basis of content, but only to give reasonable regulations concerning the "time, place, and manner" of the speech. Thus, American constitutional law as it currently exists provides a much greater protection to speech than Spinoza would have allowed. Spinoza would have placed restrictions on the *content* of speech, not only the manner of its presentation. While Spinoza's restrictions are significantly fewer than those of his contemporaries, who considered Spinoza's liberty a license for chaos, it is important to note that his view is still more restrictive than what is enjoyed in most contemporary liberal democratic societies.

While holding that some speech must be banned in a republic, Spinoza also argues that "it is impossible to deprive men of the liberty of saying what they think" (*TTP* 20.16). If it is impossible, then the sovereign does not have a right to do it. But Spinoza also argues that the sovereign must limit the right to freedom of speech to keep individuals from advocating for those dangerous beliefs that by their very nature undercut the necessary conditions for the possibility for a free society. There appears to be a deep contradiction at the very heart of Spinoza's theory of toleration. On the one side he appears to be arguing that everyone has the freedom to believe whatever he wishes and to say whatever he believes. But on the other side he argues that one cannot say or believe certain things. Is Spinoza contradicting himself? Spinoza certainly noticed the tension he creates here and attempts to address it in passages such as the following:

> If finally we remember that everyone's loyalty to the state, like their faith in God, can only be known from their works, *that is, from their charity toward their neighbor*, it will not be doubted that the best state

124 TOLERATION

> accords everyone the same liberty to philosophize as we showed that
> faith likewise allows.
>
> *(TTP* 20.9; italics added)

Here Spinoza appears to claim that one's loyalty (good will) to the state will turn entirely on the question of whether one shows charity toward one's neighbor. A charitable individual must be a loyal individual, and so not one who poses a danger to the integrity and safety of the republic. Thus, if the charitable individual is not a threat, does Spinoza hold that this individual may advocate whatever views she wishes? Spinoza indeed appears to hold that any charitable or rational individual would not advocate views that would directly undercut the necessary foundational conditions of the state. A charitable, neighborly citizen, raised by the state to be virtuous in just this way, would not advocate such ("unneighborly") ideas that would undermine the state and thereby threaten to transport the populace back into the slavery of the state of nature. In any event, the restrictions on freedom of expression are not arbitrary fiats by the sovereign, but rather must be understood as attempts by the sovereign, who has educated the citizenry in neighborly ways, to set the conditions necessary for the possibility of real freedom and growth. Again, as Spinoza famously declares:

> It is not, I contend, the purpose of the state to turn people from rational beings into beasts or automata, but rather to allow their minds and bodies to develop in their own ways in security and enjoy the free use of reason, and not to participate in conflicts based on hatred, anger or deceit or in malicious disputes with each other. Therefore, the true purpose of the state is in fact freedom.
>
> *(TTP* 20.6)

One of the central purposes of the State is to aid its citizenry to develop their minds and bodies and to overcome their passions and irrational attachments. Put slightly differently, one of the central purposes of the State is to aid its citizenry to become virtuous and so more free. Thus it appears that Spinoza is arguing that there will in fact be freedom of conscience in a state that cultivates virtue. Justice and charity are necessary for the kind of freedom of conscience that Spinoza is advocating. But how does one cultivate virtuous citizens? We turn to this question in the next section.

TOLERATION IS NECESSARY FOR A VIRTUOUS CITIZENRY

Spinoza believes that citizens must be just, tolerant, and charitable to one another for a free society to remain stable. There is nothing particularly striking about this claim. Almost all political philosophers at all times have argued that certain virtues are necessary for the state to function properly. While Spinoza's list of virtues is shorter and more "liberal" than that of most of his predecessors or contemporaries, the more innovative claim is that toleration is a necessary condition for the development of virtue in the citizenry. In its historical context this is a startling claim, and it would have seemed so to his contemporaries. Spinoza is, in effect, turning on its head a widely accepted argument made within the Christendom Model, namely, that certain kinds of *intolerance* promote virtue. Spinoza's argument was shocking to his contemporaries in much the same way that a contemporary argument for allowing young children to read or see anything without restrictions *of any kind* would be shocking to us. It is obvious that some limits are necessary if children are going to grow up well. The real debate appears to be about where exactly to mark those restrictions. The idea that intolerant, restrictive policies will in fact make citizens less virtuous is one of the most innovative aspects of Spinoza's theory of toleration. The effect of this claim is to embrace the fact that a free ("liberal") state will be a tolerant one and one that contains within itself a number of mutually exclusive views on religion, philosophy, and science. Such open-mindedness is not entirely unrestricted, for all views must conform to the structure of the Universal Religion, which as we have seen is the foundational bedrock for social life. But that is not a great restriction, given the wide latitude that we have seen Spinoza allows for the interpretation and adaption of these dogmas. The core idea remains intact: a freedom-enhancing and virtuous state must be one that allows for a number of mutually exclusive views on religion, philosophy, and science.

126 TOLERATION

Spinoza enunciates this core idea in chapter 20, the last chapter of the *Theological-Political Treatise*. He writes that "trying to control everything by laws will encourage vices rather than correcting them" (*TTP* 20.10). Suppose, Spinoza asks, that the State did attempt to control what people said. Then "men would be continually thinking one thing and saying something else. This would undermine the trust which is the first essential of the state" (*TTP* 20.11). Undermining this trust would have corrosive effects on communal life because "detestable deceit and flattery would flourish, giving rise to intrigues and destroying every kind of honest behavior" (*TTP* 20.11). Spinoza's claims here are prescient, as the history of totalitarian regimes in the twentieth century has made all too clear. One of the most objectionable features of such regimes is a constant duplicity ("doublespeak") that emerges as a response to overwhelming attempts to control. Such attempts at control create situations where citizens are forced to say one thing while thinking another. Such situations are destructive of the kind of easy trust and honesty that is foundational to the state.

Restrictive laws that limit freedom of speech and require assent to a particular (sectarian) religious dogma will also tend to cultivate intolerance in the citizenry. Such laws will make individuals more, not less, passionate and so tend to destabilize the state. Spinoza writes that:

> Such decrees as these, laying down what everyone must believe and forbidding anything from being said or written against this or that dogma, were often introduced to appease, or rather surrender to, the fury of those who cannot tolerate free minds and who, with their stern authority, easily convert the zeal of the volatile common people into rage and turn this against whomever they please.
>
> (*TTP* 20.12)

Legal restrictions and a divisive intolerance toward certain religious groups can often incite passionate hysteria and violence by partisans. Spinoza witnessed this first hand. Spinoza does not explain the exact psychological mechanisms that bring this about, but it is not difficult to see what he is getting at. Spinoza argues in the *Ethics* that a passion can only be checked by a contrary or opposite passion (*E*4p7). Thus, if a society were dominated by only one partisan group and systematically eliminated all its opponents, this group and its excesses would no longer be able to be checked. Without this check the volatile passions of the partisan group would continue to grow until they spilled over into hysterical and destructive rage. This destructive rage tends to destabilize states and causes them to respond by promulgating very restrictive laws that tend toward their own destruction. The conclusion to be drawn, that disparate groups within the state check each other's passions, is a key concept in Spinoza's defense of democracy, as we shall see in the next chapter.

In addition to cultivating dishonesty and intolerance among the citizenry, intolerant, restrictive laws are likely also to generate considerable resistance even if the policies merely prevent individuals from saying things that they believe, rather than forcing them to say things that they actually disbelieve. The more "one strives to deprive people of freedom of speech," Spinoza writes, "the more obstinately they resist" (*TTP* 20.11). Spinoza believes that it is human nature to say what one believes. Beliefs themselves cannot be controlled. While the sovereign can restrict freedom of speech, he cannot constrain beliefs on command. The greater the gap between what is believed and what is expressed in speech, the more resentment will accrue. Further, the sovereign cannot resolve this problem of the gap by means of propaganda because propaganda has never "succeeded in altogether suppressing men's awareness that they have a good deal of sense of their own and that their minds differ no less than do their palates" (*TTP* 20.2). Human vanity being what it is, and always will be, the desire to express one's (sensible) beliefs must be taken as a given. While the sovereign may attempt to "guide" the citizenry by attempting to convince them that it is best for them to defer to the sovereign authority, it is doubtful that this will succeed. The skepticism that the citizenry will develop militates against such guidance control.

Such restrictive laws are "not made to restrain the ill-intentioned so much as persecute well-meaning men, and cannot be enforced without incurring great danger to the state" (*TTP* 20.11). As we have noted above, Spinoza does in fact believe that individuals

128 TOLERATION

must express their opinions, whatever they are, in non-seditious ways, and must obey the law while objecting to it. These restrictions are required for an orderly and peaceful society. Anything beyond these restrictions crosses a dangerous line, and unjustifiably limits the opinions of "well-meaning" citizens because such restrictions have the effect of preventing good citizens from active participation in civic life and preventing them from challenging and seeking to change ineffective laws. This imperils the state. Spinoza concludes that:

> In order, then, for loyalty to be valued rather than flattery, and for sovereigns to retain their full authority and not be forced to surrender to sedition, freedom of judgment must necessarily be permitted and people must be governed in such a way that they can live in harmony, even though they openly hold different and contradictory opinions.
>
> (*TTP* 20.14)

This embrace of freedom will help to inculcate civic virtue and loyalty, which will make it possible for all to live together in harmony without the need to reach unanimity on deep questions. In addition to the political problems noted, intolerant state policies also restrict the advance of the sciences. Spinoza argues that restrictive policies are likely to cause noble and good citizens to distance themselves from the republic for fear of violating the restrictive laws (*TTP* 20.12). Thus, "liberty is absolutely essential to the advancement of the arts and sciences; for they can be cultivated with success only by those with a free and unfettered judgment" (*TTP* 20.10). As many liberal thinkers before and after Spinoza have argued, the arts and sciences can flourish only in a society that allows for reigning ideologies and dogmas to be openly challenged. Even in the fractious world of early modern Europe, Spinoza believes that a virtuous, liberal, and tolerant citizenry is instrumental for the development and sustaining of the arts and sciences.

SPINOZA AND LOCKE ON TOLERATION

We close this chapter with a brief comparison of Spinoza's views on toleration with the more famous views of John Locke. Such a

TOLERATION **129**

comparison will help to highlight what is distinctive about Spinoza's arguments. In his famous *Letter Concerning Toleration*, Locke offers essentially two arguments for the claim that "the care of souls cannot belong to the Civil Magistrate" (Locke 1983 [1689]: 26). First, Locke argues that such a policy will not work because belief is a matter of the will, not of external compulsion. Locke writes that:

> The care of Souls cannot belong to the Civil Magistrate, because his Power consists in outward force; but true and saving Religion consists in the inward perswasion of the mind, without which nothing can be acceptable to God. And such is the nature of the Understanding that it cannot be compell'd to the belief of any thing by outward force.
>
> (Locke 1983 [1689]: 27)

In this last claim both Locke and Spinoza agree. There are, however, some notable differences in how they reach this conclusion. For Locke, the saving power of religion comes about only through the individual believer's choice. One cannot compel someone to believe in a certain faith and achieve salvation thereby. Personal commitment is a key component of religion on Locke's view. Spinoza, on the other hand, does not believe in the "saving" power of any historical biblical religion, so for him "the care of souls" does not depend on faith and commitment. Rather it depends on reason and the overcoming of superstition, and this cannot be legislated in a direct way by the sovereign. Differences aside, both Locke and Spinoza agree that belief cannot be compelled or legislated, and from this a general tolerationist non-intervention concerning private opinion follows.

A second argument for toleration that Locke presents is grounded in the diversity of opinions that exist on religious matters. This diversity leads to a kind of skepticism. No one person (or institution) can reasonably claim the path to salvation, nor has anyone reason to believe that he (or it) alone possesses the whole truth and is better positioned than others to achieve salvation and eternal life. Locke writes that:

130 TOLERATION

> For there being but one Truth, one way to Heaven, what Hope is there that more Men would be led into it, if they had no Rule but the Religion of the Court, and were put under a necessity to quit the Light of their own Reason, and oppose the Dictates of their own Conscience, and blindly to resign up themselves to the Will of their Governors, and to the Religion, which either Ignorance, Ambition, or Superstition had chanced to establish in the Countries where they were born? In the variety and contradiction of Opinions in Religion, wherein the Princes of the World are as much divided as in their Secular Interests, the narrow way would be much straitned; one Country alone would be in the right, and all the rest of the World put under an obligation of following their Princes in the ways that lead to Destruction.
>
> (Locke 1983 [1689]: 28)

In this passage Locke is expressing skepticism about the wisdom of handing over to the sovereign "the care of souls", the power to impose religious beliefs on its citizenry. Locke is skeptical because the truth is so hard to discern that one cannot readily ascertain what the true path to God (salvation) is. For a start, each confessional faith offers its own exclusive path to God. Each faith offers arguments for its own exclusive correctness. These competing arguments are hard to evaluate. A healthy skepticism is prudent here. Thus, the sovereign authority should not be invested with the power to impose religious beliefs on the citizenry. Better to allow a diversity of faiths, and these considerations lead one to a general toleration with respect to religious belief.

This second argument for toleration, grounded in "the variety and contradiction of Opinions in Religion", would not move Spinoza. For him, toleration does not follow from the skepticism that attends contradictory religious beliefs, but rather from the claim that it promotes freedom. Toleration has the potential to liberate citizens, to empower them, and to make them free (rational). For Spinoza, such liberation, entrusted to the sovereign authority on behalf of his subjects, is the true "care of souls". Toleration and the virtue of tolerance are important for social and political stability, as they allow for active political engagement and a commitment to community, and also for a form of human expression that may even counter ambition and resentment. But there is also a personal side to this defense of tolerance. Spinoza's argument for toleration entails the freedom to philosophize and thereby (for a few true philosophers) the opportunity to reach human perfection (as defined in Part V of the *Ethics*). In addition to political stability for the collective, the tolerance inculcated by the state makes available for a few a life devoted to philosophy and science. In its own way, philosophy is a kind of religion with a life of its own, and Spinoza is keen to allow for this kind of life to have a place in the state.

CONCLUSION

In this chapter we have examined Spinoza's three-step argument for toleration and religious freedom. Spinoza's challenge is to argue that toleration and inclusivity can be admitted into society without the danger of social collapse. Moreover, they are instrumental for social and political stability. He supports this conclusion by arguing first that religious authority must be subject to political power. There can only be one sovereign authority in a state and that authority must be political, not religious. Second, Spinoza argues that the sovereign authority's power naturally extends only to actions and not to beliefs. The sovereign has the right to do only what is in his power to do, and no one can control the beliefs of another person. Third, Spinoza argues that intolerance and exclusivist policies breed a citizenry that is dishonest, hysterical, bigoted, and ignorant. Such a populace is not likely to be a stable one working to support a peaceful society. Toward this latter end Spinoza argues that the state should permit extensive liberties and that these liberties are necessary for the creation of a more virtuous, free, and engaged citizen. For Spinoza, religious freedom and the "freedom to philosophize may not only be allowed without danger to piety and the stability of the republic but cannot be refused without destroying the peace of the republic and piety itself" (*TTP*, title page).

132 TOLERATION

FURTHER READING

On toleration in Spinoza, see Nadler (2011, chapter 9), James (2012, chapter 12), and important articles by Rosenthal (2001b, 2003, 2008) and Steinberg (2010b). For Spinoza's criticism of the one who challenges the authority of the sovereign and the right to resist political authority, see Rosenthal (2000) and Della Rocca (2010).

7

DEMOCRATIC THEORY

INTRODUCTION

Spinoza's democratic theory pulls together all of the different strands of his thought that we have been examining in this book. His democratic theory provides a coherent alternative model of society to challenge the Christendom Model. We call this new secular and democratic model of society Liberal Republicanism. Our hope in this chapter is to reveal the overall coherence and appeal of Spinoza's view. As we saw in chapter one, the dominant approach to politics in Spinoza's day was the Christendom Model, whereby two equal but distinct partners (the Church and the State) cooperate in the project of melding a disparate group of tribes and peoples into a coherent and peaceful whole. This model of society requires a single dominant religious authority, widespread religious uniformity, and a single centralized political entity. During the early modern period this model became unworkable on account of an unprecedented increase in religious diversity alongside greater political centralization.

134 DEMOCRATIC THEORY

Let's begin our examination with a brief summary of the argument to this point. Spinoza's alternative model begins with his metaphysical naturalism, his view that one and the same set of laws governs the whole of nature. Human beings are no exception to this, and thus there are no special moral laws that apply only to human beings. Since human beings are no different in this respect from non-human animals, natural right and power are coextensive, always and everywhere. Given Spinoza's views on the nature of freedom, whereby freedom is understood as freedom from the irrational passions, leaving the pre-political state of nature for a political society makes one more, not less, free, for in the state of nature one is in bondage to the passions. Given that a political society increases one's freedom, no kind of moral justification is needed for the creation of a political society. Furthermore, on the basis of an exhaustive critique of traditional biblical religion, Spinoza undercuts any attempt to justify political power and social institutions on traditional religious foundations. On the contrary, religion is placed in the service of the state and political stability, and in the place of traditional religious dogmas – whose sectarianism is a source of deep political instability – Spinoza requires of all citizens that they share a set of general, universal religious beliefs that are consistent with and aid in the development of communal well-being. Such beliefs do not require any deep agreement on metaphysical questions and are adaptable to the variety of human types that inhabit the state. Once society is so structured and grounded, legal toleration of a diversity of views, political, religious, and philosophical, can be permitted without danger of social collapse. In fact, Spinoza argues that a general policy of toleration enhances the freedom of all by empowering all to participate in civic life. A single sovereign authority, with control over both political and religious affairs, can bring about and maintain peace in the state without requiring uniformity on contentious religious and moral issues.

But what kind of sovereign should a society have? Sovereignty, absolute political power and authority, can be held either by one person (monarchy), a small group (aristocracy), or by a large group (democracy). In the Dutch Republic in the seventeenth century all three of these possibilities were live options. The Orangists argued for monarchy with the traditional House of Orange holding supreme authority. The Statists, on the other hand, defended a more decentralized and democratic or aristocratic state. In fact, Spinoza argues that all three views are compatible with the arguments that he has laid down previously. One could accept Spinoza's views on naturalism, freedom, biblical interpretation, and toleration and at the same time combine these views with any one of the positions taken on who should hold sovereign political authority. Spinoza, however, clearly prefers some kind of democratic state because he believes that a democratic state is more equal and participatory in its structure. In this chapter we will see that Spinoza argues that a more equal society will tend to have more rational laws and so will be more stable. In this argument Spinoza turns on its head the argument for religious uniformity made by defenders of the Christendom Model. Not an enforced uniformity "from above", but the toleration of diversity within a participatory democratic state will yield the most stable and unified society.

DEMOCRACY DEFINED

Before turning to Spinoza's definition of democracy it will be useful to examine a bit more carefully why Spinoza believes that governments are necessary at all. According to Spinoza, governments have an essential role to play in human life and democratic governments play this role best. The purpose of governments is to make individuals more rational and less subject to the passions, and so more free. Spinoza writes that:

> If human beings were so constituted by nature that they desired nothing but what true reason points them to, society would surely need no laws; men would only need to learn true moral doctrine, in order to do what is truly useful of their own accord with upright and free mind. But they are not so constituted, far from it. All men do indeed seek their own interest, but it is not from the dictate of sound reason; for the most part they pursue things and judge them to be in their interest merely because they are carried away by sensual desire and their passions (which have no regard for the future and for other

136 DEMOCRATIC THEORY

> things). That is why no society can subsist without government and compulsion, and hence laws, which moderate and restrain desires.
>
> (*TTP* 5.8)

We can see in this passage why Spinoza rejects all forms of anarchism, the view that all political power is inherently illegitimate. The move from the state of nature into civil society does not corrupt and enslave the individual (as Rousseau will later argue), but perfects him by restraining his passions through the force of law. Thus, the best government would be the one with the most rational laws, those that promote moderation, justice, and charity – and so communal well-being. The Spinozistic sovereign is not a Hobbesian leviathan, enforcing the peace through the immense and overwhelming power handed to it by security-craving inhabitants of a brutal state of nature. Its role is not so much that of an enforcer as that of a "conductor" working to find the optimal way to bring about social harmony. The laws that the sovereign promulgates bind the citizens by preventing certain irrational behavior and so liberate the citizens by making their behavior more rational. It is tempting to see this conception of law as anticipating to some extent Kant and his own understanding of law-abidingness and freedom.

Spinoza believes that the best and most effective way to impose laws on a populace is through democratic means. "Democracy" can mean many different things, so it is crucial to pay careful attention to how Spinoza understands it. According to Spinoza, a democratic state is one that has popular sovereignty, an equal right to vote and be elected to office, and the rule of law. Let us examine each of these features in turn.

Spinoza argues that one has sovereignty who "makes, interprets, and repeals laws, fortifies cities, makes decisions regarding peace and war and so forth" (*PT* 2.17). A primary feature of a democratic state is that this power is held by the majority of the populace. "If this charge belongs to a council composed of the people in general," Spinoza writes, "then the state is called a democracy" (*PT* 2.17). This conception of popular sovereignty is important because, given Spinoza's views on the nature of right and power, it immediately follows that the majority in a state can do whatever

DEMOCRATIC THEORY 137

it has the power to do. Once we combine Spinoza's conception of popular sovereignty with his understanding of natural right we get his formal definition of a democratic state:

> Democracy therefore is properly defined as a united gathering of people which collectively has the sovereign right to do all that it has the power to do. It follows that sovereign power is bound by no law and everyone is obliged to obey it in all things.
>
> (*TTP* 16.8)

Because the sovereign creates the laws, it is not bound by them. It is interesting (and a little disturbing perhaps) that Spinoza grants the majority unlimited right to do anything that it can actually do. What constrains the tyranny of the majority, as John Stuart Mill would ask some two centuries later? There is no doctrine of individual rights in Spinoza that moderates or constrains the popular will. For Spinoza, if the majority decides to do something and it can in fact do it, then it possesses the right to do it. While this feature of Spinoza's democratic theory may seem frightening to contemporary readers, it is important to keep in mind those arguments offered by Spinoza, which we have already examined, that limit the sovereign power of the majority. As we noted in chapter six, Spinoza believes that there are some things that simply cannot be done by any sovereign, such as the commanding of belief. To offend against all religious sensibilities, for example, is something the sovereign will not do because it would be ineffective and potentially destabilizing. Rather the sovereign authority will work with what is given, such as a superstitious populace, to create the best society. Spinoza is a keen student of human nature, and on his view this nature provides a limiting condition on the sovereign authority, democratic or otherwise.

The second feature that Spinoza identifies with a democratic state is "the right to vote in the supreme council and to undertake offices of state" (*PT* 11.1). It is interesting that Spinoza connects these two distinct rights. The ability to participate in the supreme council and the ability to stand for public office are related rights. If one has a right to vote on the laws and to help to choose the leaders, then one must have the ability to choose whomever one

138 DEMOCRATIC THEORY

wishes, including oneself. From the right to vote in the supreme council, Spinoza can infer the right to hold public office.

But how should we understand Spinoza's invocation of "rights" in this context? We have just claimed that Spinoza does not have a doctrine of individual rights that constrains the sovereign, but now he seems to be invoking a pair of related rights that all citizens in a democratic republic possess. By "right" in this passage Spinoza seems to intend only the conception of natural right, a power or capacity, not an inalienable moral right. One has a right to vote insofar as one has the power to vote, and a democratic state is by definition one in which all citizens have this power (and so this right). Understood this way, rights cannot be conceived of as checks on sovereign power. In theory the sovereign power (the democratic majority) could vote to disenfranchise some group or class of citizens. But though it can, there may be some danger in so doing, and just such a pragmatic calculation provides a check on the sovereign's power. What we have called "weak normativity" is at work here as elsewhere in Spinoza's theorizing: while the sovereign can legitimately do whatever it is in his power to do, it does not follow that he *should*.

Finally, Spinoza lays down as a vital feature of democracy the need for a rule of law. The democratic state is one of predictable and impartially enforced laws, not one governed by the (ever-changing) will of men. Spinoza writes that:

> If it be ordained by law that the right to vote in the supreme council and to manage affairs of state should be restricted to older men who have reached a certain age, or to eldest sons as soon as they are of age, or to those who contribute a certain sum of money to the commonwealth, then although this could result in the supreme council's being composed of fewer citizens than that of the aristocracy ... yet states of this kind are still to be called democracies. because those of their citizens who are appointed to govern the commonwealth are appointed thereto not by the supreme council as being the best men, *but by law*.
> (*PT* 11.2; italics added)

The distinction between a democracy and an aristocracy in this passage rests not on how many people are part of the

DEMOCRATIC THEORY **139**

supreme council that makes the laws, but on how they got a place on the supreme council in the first place. If they got a place on this council because some peers chose them, then the state is an aristocracy. By contrast, if they got on the council by some generally applicable law, then the state is a democracy. In our view this is a somewhat convoluted claim for Spinoza to make. First, it is unclear that there is a substantive difference in the decision procedure here. If the supreme council is making the laws and these laws determine who is on the supreme council, then it appears that those on the supreme council are there because they were chosen, albeit indirectly. Likewise, aristocratic societies do not admit people to the supreme council arbitrarily but according to some rule or other (e.g., they are members of the correct family). *Prima facie* there does not seem to be a substantive difference here between aristocracy and democracy, at least on this point.

Second, the supreme council itself cannot be subject to law because the supreme council creates the laws and so is above them. As noted, the "sovereign power is bound by no law and everyone is obliged to obey it in all things" (*TTP* 16.8). If Spinoza is intending in this passage to argue that a democratic state is one that is governed by the rule of law, then he must be exempting the sovereign power from this law. Spinoza's conception of the rule of law must be quite different from our own, whereby power transfers from one person to another according to fixed impersonal rules. On our understanding the law applies inclusively, to both rulers and ruled indiscriminately. Everyone is bound by the same laws. This cannot be Spinoza's view because he holds that it is impossible for someone to bind himself.

Spinoza's definition of democracy is compatible with many different institutional structures. One can accept Spinoza's definitions and defend either a *representative republic*, in which the citizens choose the lawmakers who in turn make the laws, or a *direct democracy*, in which the citizens make the laws themselves directly. Spinoza never explicitly states a preference for one or the other. Instead he argues that while there are different types of democracy, all share the same features (*PT* 11.3). Spinoza's theorizing about the nature of democracy is at a high level of abstraction and

140 DEMOCRATIC THEORY

thus is compatible with many actual institutions depending upon the circumstances of the state at a given time.

DEMOCRATIC EQUALITY

In a democracy the citizens are subject to no one but the will of the majority, and thus no one is subject to the arbitrary will of another individual. As a result "no one transfers their natural right to another ... but rather to the majority of the whole of society of which they are a part" (*TTP* 16.11). Instead of "transferring my right" to an individual much like myself, I transfer my right/power over to a majority of which I am a small part. Spinoza thinks that this is a much more natural transfer of right/power because it preserves equality in a way that other systems of government do not. Spinoza argues that:

> In a democratic state (which is the one closest to the state of nature), all men agree, as we showed above, to act — but not to judge or think — according to the common decision. That is, because they cannot all have the same opinions, they have agreed that the view which gains the most votes should acquire the force of a decision, reserving always the right to recall their decision whenever they should find a better course.
>
> (*TTP* 20.14)

For Spinoza, democracy is the "most natural [form of government] and that which approaches most closely to the freedom nature bestows on every person" (*TTP* 16.11). What sort of "natural freedom" does Spinoza have in mind here, when he praises democracy? Further, it is not clear why, for Spinoza in particular, being akin to the state of nature is a good thing. Spinoza believes that the state of nature is a state of bondage to one's passions and a state that all rational agents will seek to escape. So why would Spinoza defend a democratic state on the grounds that it is most similar to the state of nature and so "most natural"? For Spinoza, the naturalness of the democratic state is grounded in its egalitarian and emancipatory potential. The equality that one finds in a state of nature can find its way into democracies with great advantage. Spinoza writes that:

DEMOCRATIC THEORY 141

In a democracy no one transfers their natural right to another in such a way that they are not thereafter consulted but rather to the majority of the whole society of which they are a part. In this way all remain equal as they had been previously, in the state of nature.

(*TTP* 16.11)

Spinoza wishes to preserve intact the natural equality found in the state of nature, but transform it into a stabilizing force through democratic decision-making procedures. In a state of nature natural equality is precisely the problem. Each individual has (roughly) equal power and so (roughly) equal right to do whatever he wishes. This leads to constant conflict, heightened passions, and great fear. Hobbes' solution to the conflicts and problems generated by equality seems natural – create inequality. Someone must gain complete control and impose order. Spinoza rejects Hobbes' solution and argues that the natural equality inherent in the state of nature is potentially emancipatory and can be transformed into something advantageous.

Given that the democratic state and the state of nature share this natural equality, Spinoza believes that when leaving the state of nature the potential citizenry will likely opt for democracy. In fact, Spinoza thinks that democratic equality is so natural that it is *inequality* in society that requires an explanation. Spinoza provides a tentative explanation for aristocracies in his unfinished *Political Treatise*. There he speculates that aristocratic states were once democracies because "no one willingly grants sovereignty to another" (*PT* 8.12), but an influx of foreigners to the territory, who were denied the right to vote, eventually became more numerous than the aboriginal group and tilted the balance of power in their favor. For Spinoza, there is something suspect and quite unnatural about non-democratic states.

DEMOCRATIC RATIONALITY

A more equal and participatory society will also tend to be a more rational one. The reason for this is that democratic, participatory decision-making avoids many of the idiosyncrasies of individual decision-making, and so tends toward rationality. This presumption

142 DEMOCRATIC THEORY

is perhaps surprising, given Spinoza's low assessment of the rationality of human beings, passionate and superstitious as each *individually* is. But Spinoza believes that democratic group decisions are much less subject to "the follies of appetite" (*TTP* 16.9). In a key passage Spinoza writes that "there is less reason in a democratic state to fear absurd proceedings. For it is almost impossible that the majority of a large assembly would agree on the same irrational decision" (*TTP* 16.9). Why is it almost impossible for a large assembly to agree on the same irrational decision? Spinoza seems to be suggesting here that the contrasting and opposing passions that obtain in any large assembly will tend to cancel each other out, making it unlikely that any single irrational passion will dominate. Ironically, democratic processes produce more overall rational results precisely because voters are *irrational*. Spinoza assumes that irrationality is diffused throughout the voting population. Thus, if we bring together for purposes of group decision-making a large set of random voters, Spinoza suggests that their respective passions will largely cancel each other out. The end result will be to yield decisions that are more rational than those of any one individual deciding by himself.

Further, Spinoza's psychological theory suggests that the passions, irrational as they are by their very nature, will not be randomly distributed across the population. The distribution will be "patterned", and those with similar passions may be expected to group or coalesce into different competing cliques. Grounds for this can be found at *E*3p27 where Spinoza discusses the "imitation of the affects". In this discussion Spinoza argues that we naturally sympathize with people whom we believe to be similar to ourselves and so tend to imitate their particular passions. When those similar to ourselves feel a certain passion, we tend to experience the same thing too (*E*3p27d). Thus, we would not expect that in a democratic society there would be myriad different irrational passions grounding a defense of all manner of idiosyncratic laws. Instead we would rather expect a small number of "interest groups" that would each attempt to lobby and write laws in accord with its own distinctive passion. In this way, Spinoza's political psychology predicts a system of party politics that tends toward stability, maybe even gridlock. Because the passions are randomly distributed (across

DEMOCRATIC THEORY **143**

interest groups), they will tend to cancel each other out, and the result of *this* will be an outcome more rational than that generated out of the vanity and self-regard of any one group or individual.

Canceling out or checking the passions is a positive result because it is only with respect to our passions that we differ from one another. In the *Ethics* Spinoza writes that men "can disagree in nature insofar as they are torn by affects which are passions" (E4p33). Two individuals not torn by passions, therefore, will always concur in their reasoning and so in their preferences. By canceling out the opposing passions, democratic decision-making processes bring into existence over time norms that all would have chosen if their natures were not distorted by passions. These optimally rational laws are those that all could agree on precisely because they emerge from our common (rational) nature, having winnowed out just those passions that tend to set us in opposition to each other. In our view this understanding of the emergent rational norm that guides democratic decision-making bears comparison to the notion of the General Will in Rousseau. But while Spinoza and Rousseau agree in the general approach of attempting to set up democratic procedures for producing ideal laws, they are at odds about the nature of those very procedures. Rousseau envisions a more totalitarian society where speech and action are tightly regulated so as to produce the conditions necessary for the General Will to emerge and implement the best laws. For Spinoza, by contrast, the necessary procedures are far less heavy-handed and restrictive. For a semblance of political rationality and even civic virtue to emerge from the caldron of the irrational passions, legal toleration together with the inculcation of the virtue of toleration are required. Active political engagement by all provides the very best possibility of political stability.

Spinoza's arguments here, as we have noted earlier, are similar to those made famous by Madison in *Federalist* 51. Madison defends a large republic with a powerful federal government so long as its laws are created by democratic processes. Madison argues that large and democratic societies will likely have more just laws. He claims that "by comprehending in the society so many separate descriptions of citizens" such a society "will render

144 DEMOCRATIC THEORY

an unjust combination of a majority of the whole very improbable, if not impossible" (Hamilton et al. 2010 [1788]: 290). Madison shares many of the underlying assumptions of Spinoza. He assumes that passions are spread out randomly in a population and that if we just let these competing passions check one another, we will approximate a common rationality that transcends individual distortions.

While these arguments are interesting and influential we should note that they make some assumptions about human nature and cognition that contemporary psychologists have reason to reject. The underlying assumption in Spinoza and Madison is that what all humans have in common is rationality and that the passions or irrationalities are more or less randomly diffused throughout the population. The assumption is that there are no *universal* prejudices or irrational passions that are shared by all. However, modern psychologists have concluded that this assumption is mistaken. Given the way human mental capacities have evolved over time, our minds *systematically and consistently* make irrational inferences and form beliefs on insufficient evidence (Ariely 2010; Kahneman 2011). While the study of this subject is still in its infancy, the results that have so far emerged are interesting and wide-ranging. And if true, Spinoza and Madison are likely wrong to assume that all humans share the same essential rationality and differ accidentally only in their irrational passions. We may also share common irrationalities.

RATIONALITY, STABILITY, AND FREEDOM

A state governed by rational laws will be one that is the freest and the most stable. Let us consider why such a state is a free state. The starting point is Spinoza's consistent claim that a rational person is a free person. Spinoza writes that the "only [genuinely] free person is one who lives with his entire mind guided solely by reason" (*TTP* 16.10). Reason is the basic nature and structure of the human mind, according to Spinoza, and so rational laws are the governing laws of one's mind. When one is rational, one is not compelled or enslaved by an outside force, like the passions, which by their nature are external to our (rational) nature. So

DEMOCRATIC THEORY **145**

liberated from the passions, one is free and autonomous. Such naturalism helps Spinoza avoid a paradox related to the very nature of government. Governments promulgate laws and force citizens to follow them. Can citizens be both compelled and free at the same time? Spinoza (along with Rousseau) answers, "Yes". Spinoza writes that:

> Acting on command, that is, from obedience, does take away liberty in some sense, but it is not acting on command in itself that makes someone a slave, but rather the reason for so acting. If the purpose of the action is not his own advantage but that of his ruler, then the agent is indeed a slave and useless to himself ... The freest state, therefore, is that whose laws are founded on sound reason; for there each man can be free whenever he wishes, that is, he can live under the guidance of reason with his whole mind.
>
> *(TTP* 16.10)

According to Spinoza, one can be compelled *and* free. When the laws command on the basis of "sound reason", one is commanded to be free because one is enjoined to behave *as if* one were rational. This is a clear benefit to the irrational person, who may over time acquire the habit for acting rationally. In this way, the law molds irrational citizens. It is a helpful regimen. Consider: if someone is severely ill, perhaps mentally ill, and does not wish to take medication for the illness, then a nurse or doctor may have to force the patient to take the medicine *for his own good*. Being forced to take the medication does not make the patient less free. His freedom not to take the medication is no freedom at all, according to this account, precisely because it is contrary to his own good. In doing what is actually in the best interest of the patient, the nurse or doctor is attempting to liberate (free) the patient from the mania that currently enslaves him. The patient's sickness, not his rational nature, is the culprit and the cause for resisting the required dosing. It is this sickness (analogous to the passions) that is enslaving the patient and causing him to continue to be in bondage to the illness. When the nurse counters the resistance and forces the medicine down his throat, then the patient is advantaged.

146 DEMOCRATIC THEORY

The paternalism in Spinoza's system is not, however, one class ruling over another. In coming to recognize that we are *all* suffering from the sickness of the passions, trust in collective decision-making, rather than our own distorted reasoning, emerges as the antidote to our individual irrationality. The paternalism on offer here leads only to the conclusion that we ought to trust more in collective decision-making than in any hierarchical authority. In a democratic state governed by rational and good laws, the state may reasonably demand that the laws be followed, even as they *appear* to constrain us. "In such a society," Spinoza writes, "whether the number of laws is increased or reduced, the people still remain just as free, since they are not acting under the authority of another but by their own proper consent" (*TTP* 5.9). The "consent" referred to in this passage is analogous to the nurse in the aforementioned example, who may be said to be acting with the patient's "consent" in the sense that she is acting in the patient's best interest. The state enforces obedience to its laws, and when those laws are rational and in the citizens' best interests, then the laws make the citizens freer, precisely because they make the citizens more rational and less prone to the destabilizing powers of passionate rhetoric, etc. Since democratic states will have more rational laws, democratic states will be the most free. Spinoza concludes with a famous remark: "the true purpose of the state is in fact freedom" (*TTP* 20.6).

"The opposite is the case," Spinoza warns, "when one man alone holds power absolutely" (*TTP* 5.9). The problem in such a case is not the fact that just one person is holding power and forcing others to obey his rules. Such a situation could, at least in theory, make individuals more free. The problem is that the rules promulgated by just one ruler (a monarch) are likely to only be partly rational, less than optimally so, because the law will conform to his own particular psychology – passions and all – rather than to rational nature as such. The result may not be in the best interests of the citizens. Forcing the citizens to obey these less than optimally rational laws will in fact make them less free because they will be forced to follow, contrary to their best interests, the irrational, self-regarding, edicts of the ruler. This is why Spinoza thinks that

DEMOCRATIC THEORY **147**

monarchies lend themselves more often to enslavement of the populace, while democracies tend to liberate their citizenry. With this increase in autonomy-enhancing freedom comes the possibility of significant negative liberty too. The more rational the population, the fewer the number of laws that will be necessary to keep the citizenry in check. The better the government does its job, the less the government will have to do.

There will also be fewer conflicts in a rational society. "Only insofar as men live according to the guidance of reason," Spinoza writes, "must they always agree in nature" (*E*4p35). As individuals become freer they tend to harmonize with one another, with the result that fewer conflicts arise. Conflicts between people, Spinoza argues, will never come about from a shared consensus, but only from differences. Likewise, the greater the rational consensus that exists in a republic, the freer, more like-minded, and peaceful the citizens will become. Law-abidingness is a function of rational agreement and virtue.

It is for all of these reasons that "a man who is guided by reason is more free in a state, where he lives according to a common decision, than in solitude, where he obeys only himself" (*E*4p73). His freedom comes from two different effects that the state brings about. First, the State will likely help to compensate for the residual irrationalities of the generally rational person. Spinoza claims in the *Ethics* that no one can be thoroughly rational (only God is), with the result that no one is ever fully devoid of the passions (*E*4p4c). In recognition of such weaknesses and parochial idiosyncrasies, a rational agent will seek to cooperate in friendship with others for the sake of his own well-being and freedom. And a democratic state is particularly advantageous in this regard because in it one finds a greater number of individuals who are politically enfranchised, and hence participants in the reason-guiding goals of political life. Second, the State advances the freedom of all, and in so advancing a rational outlook, the State creates an arena in which the rational agent finds common ground with his fellow countrymen. Given Spinoza's views on the "imitation of the affects", which we have noted, this common ground will help each citizen to sympathize more easily with one's fellows. This increased sympathy will then lessen competing factions within society and help to forge a more

148 DEMOCRATIC THEORY

coherent and unified society. In sum, the more rational a society, the fewer the competing factions that obtain in that society, and that is advantageous for everyone.

LIBERAL REPUBLICANISM: FROM DIVERSITY TO UNITY

Before we conclude our examination of Spinoza's alternative to the Christendom Model, let us first briefly summarize the reasoning to this point. Spinoza's argument for the superiority of democracy over other forms of government begins with the claim that it makes individuals more equal. This equality is necessary because it gives each citizen more power to help shape the laws. This fact in turn helps to make the laws more rational. More rational laws make individuals more free. Freer people are more similar to one another. Those who are similar to one another have fewer conflicts. Thus, a free society is a more stable society.

Prima facie there seems to be a tension between (i) the toleration of diversity and factionalism, which Spinoza argues is necessary in a democratic state, and (ii) the requirement of unanimity, which Spinoza believes is the result of rationality. Strange as the view may initially appear, Spinoza believes that tolerating diversity is necessary because (in a properly democratic state) it results in a true civic unity, which is not to be confused with a half-hearted conformity. For Spinoza, such unity is the *summum bonum*, and diversity is not in itself desirable. In this conclusion, Spinoza is in *formal* agreement with his contemporaries who argue for religious uniformity. However, Spinoza differs from his contemporaries in arguing that democratic processes, not religious theocracies, are the best vehicle to harness and streamline destabilizing diversity and to bring about a unifying consensus that becomes a stabilizing force in the state.

Keeping in mind this preference for democracy and democratic processes, and their ameliorating tendencies, we conclude by examining a central element of Spinoza's political model, his theory of public virtues. Spinoza's analysis of the virtues, and their inculcation, in political life stakes out a middle ground between classical liberalism and classical republicanism. Though often assimilated

DEMOCRATIC THEORY **149**

to Hobbes, Spinoza is not a liberal in the manner of Hobbes, for he holds that the State has a positive role to play in the lives of its citizens as a teacher of virtue, and, further, he holds that the freedom that is the *summum bonum* is not negative (or libertarian) freedom.

Spinoza, however, is not a classical republican in the mold of Machiavelli or Rousseau. Recall:

> It is not, I contend, the purpose of the state to turn people from rational beings into beasts or automata, but rather to allow their minds and bodies to develop in their own ways in security and enjoy the free use of reason, and not to participate in conflicts based on hatred, anger or deceit or in malicious disputes with each other. Therefore, the true purpose of the state is in fact freedom.
>
> (*TTP* 20.6)

This description of the role of the State in directing its citizens to the good is more nuanced than those classical republican theories whose public policies are built on a homogeneity grounded in a shared ideological consensus. We call Spinoza's position Liberal Republicanism, and it is one of the more interesting aspects of his democratic theory. The basic idea behind Spinoza's Liberal Republicanism is that in order to enable democracies to create unity from diversity, citizens need to cultivate a certain set of (thin) virtues, indeed those very virtues embedded in the public dogmas of the Universal Religion. First, they need to develop the virtues that are required to accommodate diversity in the state without destabilizing the state. Such accommodation requires that citizens cultivate virtues such as tolerance. This virtue is the virtue of the acceptance of differences and resisting the temptation to suppress those differences. Difficult as it is to fully embrace such diversity, Spinoza believes citizens can be taught to accept or tolerate it in the spirit of the Golden Rule. In addition to tolerance, citizens in Spinoza's liberal republic will need to develop the virtue of justice. This is a virtue that presupposes some kind of equality under the law, a virtue of rendering unto each his own. The promotion of the virtues of tolerance and justice allow the diversity of the democratic state to

150 DEMOCRATIC THEORY

be peacefully sustained and enhanced during the time it takes to create the laws.

Further, the State must aid each citizen in developing those virtues that help to mold them into more rational individuals. This will be of benefit both for the individual and for the State itself, whose self-interest in loyalty and obedience is obvious. It is no surprise that Spinoza highly values the virtue of obedience in his Universal Religion (*TTP* 14.5; 14.11). In context, obedience is the virtue of accepting in an agreeable way the laws of the State because in so obeying good laws one *ipso facto* engages in a practice that unites one citizen with another, to the benefit of each and all. Obedience here is not blind, but a willing acceptance of the public rule. Perhaps we may say that it is with the virtues of tolerance and justice that we work to make the laws, and then with the virtue of obedience we adopt them.

We call these virtues of tolerance, justice, and obedience "thin" or liberal virtues. They are formal, procedural, and universal. They are not parochial and do not promote a specific way of life, but only rule out ways of life that involve intolerance, injustice, and reckless individualism. This set of liberal virtues may be contrasted with a more robust list of republican virtues. Classical republicanism incentivizes virtues such as patriotism or Christian piety, which are focused on particular states or religious confessions. Classical republicanism entails significant constraints on negative liberty because it understands the role of the State as molding citizens whose horizons do not extend beyond it. While Spinoza, liberals, and classical republicans all see the absolute necessity of the State, only Spinoza combines a commitment to democratic freedom and diversity with a belief that just this commitment provides a foundation for the development over time of a kind of citizen who is rational and dispassionate.

Spinoza's democratic theory pulls together all of the different strands of his thought. It provides innovative answers to the two major political problems facing Spinoza and his contemporaries, which we have discussed throughout this book. It is fitting then that we close this book with a brief exploration of Spinoza's answers to these most pressing problems of his age: the Problem of Political Legitimacy and the Problem of Cooperation without Agreement.

DEMOCRATIC THEORY 151

The first question that Spinoza's contemporaries face with the collapse of the Christendom Model is this: Without religion as the foundation, how is a legitimate ruler distinguished from an illegitimate one? Spinoza's answer is that a legitimate ruler is one who makes the citizens more free, by instituting and enforcing obedience to rational, freedom-enhancing, laws. For Spinoza, this leads directly to democracy and democratic institutions, as the processes whereby freedom is enhanced and the legitimacy of the sovereign is guaranteed. It is important to note that the grounds of such legitimacy sever political legitimacy from deep questions of religion or morality, as is required in the Christendom Model. Diversity, therefore, can no longer be thought to undermine political legitimacy.

The second question that arises with the collapse of the Christendom Model is this: How much peaceful cooperation is possible without deep agreement on fundamental questions? Spinoza answers that peaceful cooperation is possible if the citizens are tolerant, just, and obedient. These virtues make peaceful cooperation possible by allowing the democratic processes to function. Thus, the more tolerant, just, and obedient each person is, the more rational and free that person will become over time. This rationality will in turn make possible even greater levels of cooperation. One does not require unanimity of belief, even on deep questions, in order to make democratic processes work, because these processes are not legitimated by reference to religion or morality. Spinoza believes that democratic processes will tend over time to create a certain unanimity, a shared consensus, as citizens come to develop a rational and dispassionate outlook. Spinoza resolves the central political problem of his age by turning diversity into an asset rather than a liability.

CONCLUSION

In this final chapter we have examined Spinoza's democratic theory and the role that virtue plays in his system. Spinoza is a keen observer of human nature, and a realist about its prospects. We argued that for Spinoza democracy is the best form of government precisely because human beings are by nature subject to fear and superstition. The challenge for Spinoza is to create and

DEMOCRATIC THEORY

sustain a political system that turns a natural diversity and disagreeableness into a shared consensus, without resorting to sectarian violence or mind control. To make this happen the State needs to help its citizens cultivate the liberal virtues of tolerance, justice, and obedience. Cultivating these virtues will allow for a healthy testing of ideas and a stern demand for accountability from all citizens. Spinoza believes that over time the political arena will see less volatility, to the advantage of all. Political legitimacy may now be understood as deriving not from transcendent norms or on the basis of contractual obligations, but rather from the cultivation of freedom and rational insight, which themselves are the result of a moderated diversity. Spinoza believes that the State has a compelling interest in sustaining diversity, for in becoming a true laboratory of ideas, it advances the freedom of all.

FURTHER READING

Spinoza's Liberal Republicanism, which promotes a positive role for the State in the inculcation of a set of distinctively liberal virtues in the citizenry and its liberation, is discussed in Steinberg (2008, 2009) and Rosenthal (2003). Rosenthal (1998) and Steinberg (2010a) discuss collective action problems in Spinoza, in which self- and group-interests coincide and conflict, and the nature, and advantages, of democratic deliberative processes. For a somewhat similar argument in Aristotle (in *Politics* 3.11) about the inherent "rationality" or wisdom of the "many" and their collective views, see Waldron (1995).

BIBLIOGRAPHY

TEXTS AND TRANSLATIONS

Aquinas, Thomas. *Summa Theologiae*, trans. English Dominicans. London: Burns, Oates, and Washbourne, 1912–36.

Austin, John. *The Province of Jurisprudence Determined*, ed. W. Rumble. Cambridge: Cambridge University Press, 1995.

Bodin, Jean. *On Sovereignty*, trans. J. H. Franklin. Cambridge: Cambridge University Press, 1992.

Descartes, René. *Meditations on First Philosophy*, trans. D. Cress. Indianapolis: Hackett, 1993.

Grotius, Hugo. *Prolegomena to the Law of War and Peace*, trans. F. W. Kelsey. Indianapolis: Bobbs-Merrill, 1955.

Hamilton, Alexander, James Madison, and John Jay. *The Federalist Papers*. Charleston, SC: Tribeca Books, 2010.

Hobbes, Thomas. *Leviathan*, ed. E. Curley. Indianapolis: Hackett, 1994.

——. *On the Citizen*, ed. and trans. R. Tuck and M. Silverthorne. Cambridge: Cambridge University Press, 1998.

Hooker, Richard. *Of the Laws of Ecclesiastical Polity*, ed. A. S. McGrade. Cambridge: Cambridge University Press, 1989.

Hume, David. *An Enquiry Concerning Human Understanding*, ed. E. Steinberg. Indianapolis: Hackett, 1993.

——. *Dialogues Concerning Natural Religion*, ed. R. H. Popkin. Indianapolis: Hackett, 1998.

Locke, John. *Second Treatise on Government*, ed. C. B. Macpherson. Indianapolis: Hackett, 1980.

154 BIBLIOGRAPHY

——. *A Letter Concerning Toleration*, ed. J. H. Tully. Indianapolis: Hackett, 1983.

Machiavelli, Niccolo. *The Prince*, ed. and trans. Q. Skinner and R. Price. Cambridge: Cambridge University Press, 1988.

Meyer, Lodewijk. *Philosophy as the Interpreter of Holy Scripture*, trans. S. Shirley. Milwaukee, WI: Marquette University Press, 2005 (orig. 1966).

Rousseau, Jean-Jacques. *"The Discourses" and Other Early Political Writings*, ed. and trans. V. Gourevitch. Cambridge: Cambridge University Press, 1997.

——. *"The Social Contract" and Other Later Political Writings*, ed. and trans. V. Gourevitch. Cambridge: Cambridge University Press, 1997.

Spinoza, Baruch/Benedictus de. *Spinoza Opera*, ed. C. Gebhardt, 4 vols. Heidelberg: Carl Winter, 1925.

——. *The Political Works*, ed. and trans. A. G. Wernham. Oxford: Clarendon Press, 1958.

——. *The Collected Works of Spinoza*, trans. E. Curley, vol. 1. Princeton: Princeton University Press, 1985.

——. *Political Treatise*, trans. S. Shirley. Indianapolis: Hackett, 2000.

——. *Spinoza: Complete Works*, ed. M. L. Morgan; trans. S. Shirley. Indianapolis: Hackett, 2002.

——. *Theological-Political Treatise*, ed. and trans. J. Israel and M. Silverthorne. Cambridge: Cambridge University Press, 2007.

OTHER BOOKS AND ARTICLES

Adkins, Brent. *True Freedom: Spinoza's Practical Philosophy*. New York: Lexington Books, 2009.

Ariely, Dan. *Predictably Irrational: The Hidden Forces That Shape Our Decisions*. New York: Harper, 2010.

Armstrong, Aurelia. "Natural and Unnatural Communities: Spinoza beyond Hobbes". *British Journal for the History of Philosophy* 17: 279–305, 2009.

Bagley, Paul. *Philosophy, Theology, and Politics: A Reading of Benedict Spinoza's Tractatus Theologico-Politicus*. Leiden: Brill, 2008.

Barbone, Steven and Lee Rice. "Spinoza and the Problem of Suicide." *International Philosophical Quarterly* 34: 229–41, 1994.

Beiner, Ronald. *Civil Religion: A Dialogue in the History of Political Philosophy*. Cambridge: Cambridge University Press, 2010.

Bennett, Jonathan. *A Study of Spinoza's Ethics*. Indianapolis: Hackett, 1984.

Berlin, Isaiah. "Two Concepts of Liberty." In *Four Essays on Liberty*. London: Oxford University Press: 118–73, 1969.

Blom, Hans. "The Moral and Political Philosophy of Spinoza." In *The Renaissance and Seventeenth-century Rationalism*, ed. G. H. R. Parkinson. London: Routledge: 313–48, 1993.

——. "Spinoza on *Res Publica*, Republics, and Monarchies." In *Monarchisms in the Age of Enlightenment: Liberty, Patriotism, and the Common Good*, ed. H. Blom, J. C. Laursen, and L. Simonutti. Toronto: University of Toronto Press: 19–44, 2007.

BIBLIOGRAPHY 155

Bokenkotter, Thomas. *A Concise History of the Catholic Church*. New York: Doubleday, 2004.

Bonney, Richard. *The Thirty Years' War: 1618–1648*. Oxford: Osprey Publishing, 2002.

Cohen, Joshua. "An Epistemic Basis of Democracy." *Ethics* 97: 26–38, 1986.

Collinson, Patrick. *The Reformation: A History*. New York: Random House, 2006.

Curley, Edwin. "Spinoza's Moral Philosophy." In *Spinoza: A Collection of Critical Essays*, ed. M. Grene. Garden City, NY: Anchor: 354–76, 1973.

——. "Notes on a Neglected Masterpiece (II): The *Theological-Political Treatise* as a Prolegomenon to the *Ethics*." In *Central Themes in Early Modern Philosophy*, ed. J. A. Cover and M. Kulstad. Indianapolis: Hackett: 109–60, 1990.

——. "The State of Nature and Its Law in Hobbes and Spinoza." *Philosophical Topics* 19: 97–117, 1991.

——. "'I Durst Not Write So Boldly,' or How to Read Hobbes' Theological-Political Treatise." In *Hobbes e Spinoza, scienza e politica*, ed. D. Bostrenghi. Naples: Bibliopolis: 497–593, 1992.

——. "Notes on a Neglected Masterpiece (I): Spinoza and the Science of Hermeneutics." In *Spinoza: The Enduring Questions*, ed. G. Hunter. Toronto: University of Toronto Press: 64–99, 1994.

——. "Kissinger, Spinoza, and Genghis Khan." In *The Cambridge Companion to Spinoza*, ed. D. Garrett. Cambridge: Cambridge University Press: 315–42, 1996.

Dagger, Richard. *Civic Virtues: Rights, Citizenship, and Republican Liberalism*. Oxford: Oxford University Press, 1997.

De Dijn, Herman. "Spinoza on Truth, Religion, and Salvation." *Review of Metaphysics* 66: 545–64, 2013.

Della Rocca, Michael. "Getting His Hands Dirty: Spinoza's Criticism of the Rebel." In *Spinoza's Theological-Political Treatise: A Critical Guide*, ed. Y. Melamed and M. Rosenthal. Cambridge: Cambridge University Press: 168–91, 2010.

Den Uyl, Douglas J. *Power, State and Freedom: An Interpretation of Spinoza's Political Philosophy*. Assen, The Netherlands: Van Gorcum, 1983.

——. "Sociality and Social Contract: A Spinozistic Perspective." *Studia Spinozana* 1: 19–51, 1985.

Eckstein, Walter. "Rousseau and Spinoza: Their Political Theories and Their Conception of Ethical Freedom." *Journal of the History of Ideas* 5: 259–91, 1944.

Estlund, David. "Beyond Fairness and Deliberation: The Epistemic Dimension of Democratic Authority." In *Deliberative Democracy: Essays on Reason and Politics*, ed. J. Bohman and W. Rehg. Cambridge, MA: MIT Press: 173–204, 1997.

Feuer, Lewis. *Spinoza and the Rise of Liberalism*. Boston: Beacon Press, 1958.

Frankel, Steven. "Politics and Rhetoric: The Intended Audience of Spinoza's *Tractatus Theologico-Politicus*." *Review of Metaphysics* 52: 897–924, 1999.

——. "The Invention of Liberal Theology: Spinoza's Theological-Political Analysis of Moses and Jesus." *Review of Politics* 63: 287–315, 2001.

——. "The Piety of a Heretic: Spinoza's Interpretation of Judaism." *Journal of Jewish Thought and Philosophy* 11: 117–34, 2002.

Galston, William. *Liberal Purposes: Goods, Virtues, and Diversity in the Liberal State*. Cambridge: Cambridge University Press, 1991.

BIBLIOGRAPHY

Garber, Daniel. "Dr. Fischelson's Dilemma: Spinoza on Freedom and Sociability." In *Spinoza by 2000: The Jerusalem Conferences. Ethica IV: Spinoza on Reason and the "Free Man"*, ed. Y. Yovel and G. Segal. New York: Little Room Press: 183–208, 2004.

Garrett, Aaron. "Was Spinoza a Natural Lawyer?" *Cardozo Law Review* 25: 627–41, 2003.

Garrett, Don. "'A Free Man Always Acts Honestly, not Deceptively': Freedom and the Good in Spinoza's Ethics." In *Spinoza: Issues and Directions*, ed. E. Curley and P.-F. Moreau. Leiden: Brill: 221–38, 1990.

——. "Spinoza's Ethical Theory." In *The Cambridge Companion to Spinoza*, ed. D. Garrett. Cambridge: Cambridge University Press: 267–314, 1996.

——. "Spinoza's *Conatus* Argument." In *Spinoza: Metaphysical Themes*, ed. O. Koistinen and J. Biro. Oxford: Oxford University Press: 127–58, 2002.

——. "'Promising' Ideas: Hobbes and Contract in Spinoza's Political Philosophy." In *Spinoza's Theological-Political Treatise: A Critical Guide*, ed. Y. Melamed and M. Rosenthal. Cambridge: Cambridge University Press: 192–209, 2010.

Gatens, Moira. "Spinoza's Disturbing Thesis: Power, Norms and Fiction in the *Tractatus Theologico-Politicus*." *History of Political Thought* 30: 455–68, 2009.

——. and Genevieve Lloyd. *Collective Imaginings: Spinoza, Past and Present*. London: Routledge, 1999.

Halper, Edward. "Spinoza on the Political Value of Freedom of Religion." *History of Philosophy Quarterly* 21: 167–82, 2004.

Hampshire, Stuart. *Spinoza and Spinozism*. Oxford: Clarendon Press, 2005.

Hart, H. L. A. *The Concept of Law*. Oxford: Oxford University Press, 1961.

Hollister, Warren et al. (ed.). *Medieval Europe: A Short Sourcebook*, 4th edition. New York: McGraw-Hill, 2002.

Holmes, Stephen. *Passions and Constraint: On the Theory of Liberal Democracy*. Chicago: University of Chicago Press, 1995.

Hurka, Thomas. *Perfectionism*. Oxford: Oxford University Press, 1993.

Israel, Jonathan. "The Intellectual Debate about Toleration in the Dutch Republic." In *The Emergence of Tolerance in the Dutch Republic*, ed. C. Berkvens-Stevelinck, J. Israel, and G. H. M. Posthumus Meyjes. Leiden: Brill: 3–36, 1997.

——. "Spinoza, Locke, and the Enlightenment Battle for Toleration." In *Toleration in Enlightenment Europe*, ed. O. P. Grell and R. Porter. Cambridge: Cambridge University Press: 102–13, 2000.

——. *Radical Enlightenment: Philosophy and the Making of Modernity, 1650–1750*. Oxford: Oxford University Press, 2001.

——. "The Intellectual Origins of Modern Democratic Republicanism (1660–1720)." *European Journal of Political Theory* 3: 7–36, 2004.

——. *Enlightenment Contested: Philosophy, Modernity, and the Emancipation of Man 1670–1752*. Oxford: Oxford University Press, 2006.

James, Susan. "Power and Difference: Spinoza's Conception of Freedom." *Journal of Political Philosophy* 4: 207–28, 1996.

——. "Narrative as the Means to Freedom: Spinoza on the Uses of Imagination." In *Spinoza's Theological-Political Treatise: A Critical Guide*, ed. Y. Melamed and M. Rosenthal. Cambridge: Cambridge University Press: 250–67, 2010.

BIBLIOGRAPHY **157**

———. *Spinoza on Philosophy, Religion, and Politics: The Theologico-Political Treatise*. Oxford: Oxford University Press, 2012.

Kahneman, Daniel. *Thinking, Fast and Slow*. New York: Farrar, Straus and Giroux, 2011.

Kisner, Matthew. *Spinoza on Human Freedom: Reason, Autonomy and the Good Life*. Cambridge: Cambridge University Press, 2011.

Laursen, John Christian. "Spinoza on Toleration." In *Difference and Dissent: Theories of Tolerance in Medieval and Early Modern Europe*, ed. C. J. Nederman and J. C. Laursen. Lanham, MD: Rowman & Littlefield: 185–204, 1996.

LeBuffe, Michael. *From Bondage to Freedom: Spinoza on Human Excellence*. Oxford: Oxford University Press, 2010.

MacCulloch, Diarmaid. *The Reformation: A History*. New York: Penguin Books, 2005.

Macherey, Pierre. "A Propos de la différence entre Hobbes et Spinoza." In *Hobbes e Spinoza, scienza e politica*, ed. D. Bostrenghi. Naples: Bibliopolis: 689–98, 1992.

Malcolm, Noel. "Hobbes and Spinoza." In *The Cambridge History of Political Thought, 1450–1700*, ed. J. H. Burns. Cambridge: Cambridge University Press: 530–57, 1991.

Martinich, A. P. *The Two Gods of Leviathan: Thomas Hobbes on Religion and Politics*. Cambridge: Cambridge University Press, 1992.

Matheron, Alexandre. *Individu et Communauté chez Spinoza*. Paris: Les Éditions de Minuit, 1969.

———. "Le problème de l'évolution de Spinoza du *Traité théologico-politique* au *Traité politique*." In *Spinoza: Issues and Directions*, ed. E. Curley and P.-F. Moreau. Leiden: Brill: 258–70, 1990.

———. "The Theoretical Function of Democracy in Spinoza and Hobbes." In *The New Spinoza*, ed. W. Montag and T. Stolze. Minneapolis: University of Minnesota Press: 207–17, 1997.

McGrath, Alister. *A Fine-Tuned Universe: The Quest for God in Science and Theology*. Louisville, KY: Westminster John Knox Press, 2009.

McShea, Robert. *The Political Philosophy of Spinoza*. New York: Columbia University Press, 1968.

Melamed, Yitzhak and Michael Rosenthal (eds.). *Spinoza's Theological-Political Treatise: A Critical Guide*. Cambridge: Cambridge University Press, 2010.

Miller, Jon. "Spinoza and the Concept of a Law of Nature." *History of Philosophy Quarterly* 20: 257–76, 2003.

———. "Spinoza and Natural Law." In *Reason, Religion, and Natural Law: From Plato to Spinoza*, ed. J. Jacobs. Oxford: Oxford University Press: 201–21, 2012.

Nadler, Steven. *Spinoza: A Life*. Cambridge: Cambridge University Press, 1999.

———. "Hope, Fear, and the Politics of Immortality." In *Analytic Philosophy and History of Philosophy*, ed. T. Sorell and G. A. J. Rogers. Oxford: Clarendon Press: 201–17, 2005.

———. "Baruch Spinoza and the Naturalization of Judaism." In *The Cambridge Companion to Modern Jewish Philosophy*, ed. M. L. Morgan and P. Gordon. Cambridge: Cambridge University Press: 14–34, 2007.

158 BIBLIOGRAPHY

———. *A Book Forged in Hell: Spinoza's Scandalous Treatise and the Birth of the Secular Age*. Princeton: Princeton University Press, 2011.

Nexon, Daniel. *The Struggle for Power in Early Modern Europe: Religious Conflict, Dynastic Empires, and International Change*. Princeton: Princeton University Press, 2009.

Nussbaum, Martha. *Liberty of Conscience: In Defense of America's Tradition of Religious Equality*. New York: Basic Books, 2010.

Parkinson, G. H. R. "Spinoza on the Freedom of Man and the Freedom of the Citizen." In *Conceptions of Liberty in Political Philosophy*, ed. Z. Pelczynski and J. Gray. London: St. Martin's Press: 39–56, 1984.

Pines, Shlomo. "Spinoza's *Tractatus Theologico-Politicus*, Maimonides, and Kant." In *Studies in the History of Jewish Thought*, ed W. Z. Harvey and M. Idel. Jerusalem: Magnes Press: 660–711, 1997.

Pinker, Steven. *Better Angels of Our Nature: Why Violence Has Declined*. New York: Viking Press, 2011.

Pocock, J. G. A. *The Machiavellian Moment: Florentine Political Thought and the Atlantic Republican Tradition*. Princeton: Princeton University Press, 1975.

Popkin, Richard. "Spinoza and Bible Scholarship." In *The Cambridge Companion to Spinoza*, ed. D. Garrett. Cambridge: Cambridge University Press: 383–407, 1996.

Prak, Maarten. *The Dutch Republic in the Seventeenth Century: The Golden Age*. Cambridge: Cambridge University Press, 2005.

Preus, J. Samuel. *Spinoza and the Irrelevance of Biblical Authority*. Cambridge: Cambridge University Press, 2001.

Prokhovnik, Raia. *Spinoza and Republicanism*. London and New York: Palgrave Macmillan, 2004.

Raphael, D. D. "The Intolerable." In *Justifying Toleration*, ed. S. Mendus. Cambridge: Cambridge University Press: 137–53, 1988.

Raz, Joseph. *The Morality of Freedom*. Oxford: Clarendon Press, 1986.

Richardson, Lewis. *Statistics of Deadly Quarrels*. Pittsburgh: Boxwood Press, 1960.

Rosenthal, Michael. "Why Spinoza Chose the Hebrews: The Exemplary Function of Prophecy in the *Theological-Political Treatise*." *History of Political Thought* 18: 207–41, 1997.

———. "Two Collective Action Problems in Spinoza's Social Contract Theory." *History of Philosophy Quarterly* 15: 389–409, 1998.

———. "Toleration and the Right to Resist in Spinoza's *Theological-Political Treatise*: The Problem of Christ's Disciples." In *Piety, Peace and the Freedom to Philosophize*, ed. P. Bagley. Dordrecht: Kluwer: 111–32, 2000.

———. "Spinoza's Dogmas of Universal Faith and the Problem of Religion." *Philosophy & Theology* 13: 53–72, 2001a.

———. "Tolerance as a Virtue in Spinoza's *Ethics*." *Journal of the History of Philosophy* 39: 535–57, 2001b.

———. "Spinoza's Republican Argument for Toleration." *Journal of Political Philosophy* 11: 320–37, 2003.

———. "Spinoza on Why the Sovereign Can Command Men's Tongues but Not Their Minds." In *Nomos* 48, "Toleration and Its Limits", ed. M. Williams and J. Waldron. New York: New York University Press: 54–77, 2008.

BIBLIOGRAPHY 159

——. "Miracles, Wonder, and the State in Spinoza's *Theological-Political Treatise*." In *Spinoza's Theological-Political Treatise: A Critical Guide*, ed. Y. Melamed and M. Rosenthal. Cambridge: Cambridge University Press: 231–49, 2010.

Russell, Paul. *The Riddle of Hume's Treatise: Skepticism, Naturalism, and Irreligion*. Oxford: Oxford University Press, 2010.

Rutherford, Donald. "Spinoza and the Dictates of Reason." *Inquiry* 51: 485–511, 2008.

——. "Spinoza's Conception of Law: Metaphysics and Ethics." In *Spinoza's Theological-Political Treatise: A Critical Guide*, ed. M. Rosenthal and Y. Melamed and M. Rosenthal. Cambridge: Cambridge University Press: 143–67, 2010.

Sher, George. *Beyond Neutrality: Perfectionism and Politics*. Cambridge: Cambridge University Press, 1997.

——. "Freedom of Expression in the Non-Neutral State." In *Perfectionism and Neutrality: Essays in Liberal Theory*, ed. S. Wall and G. Klosko. Lanham, MD: Rowman & Littlefield: 219–30, 2003.

Smith, Steven B. *Spinoza, Liberalism, and the Question of Jewish Identity*. New Haven: Yale University Press, 1997.

Steinberg, Diane. "Spinoza's Ethical Doctrine and the Unity of Human Nature." *Journal of the History of Philosophy* 22: 303–24, 1984.

Steinberg, Justin. "On Being Sui Iuris: Spinoza and the Republican Idea of Liberty." *History of European Ideas* 34: 239–49, 2008.

——. "Spinoza on Civil Liberation." *Journal of the History of Philosophy* 47: 35–58, 2009.

——. "Benedict Spinoza: Epistemic Democrat." *History of Philosophy Quarterly* 27: 145–64, 2010a.

——. "Spinoza's Curious Defense of Toleration." In *Spinoza's Theological-Political Treatise: A Critical Guide*, ed. Y. Melamed and M. Rosenthal. Cambridge: Cambridge University Press: 210–30, 2010b.

——. "Spinoza's Political Philosophy." In *The Stanford Encyclopedia of Philosophy* (2013). http://plato.stanford.edu/archives/win2013/entries/spinoza-political/

Strauss, Leo. *Spinoza's Critique of Religion*, trans. E. M. Sinclair. Chicago: University of Chicago Press, 1965.

Te Brake, Wayne. *Shaping History: Ordinary People in European Politics 1500–1700*. Berkeley: University of California Press, 1998.

Tuck, Richard. *Natural Rights Theories: Their Origin and Development*. New York: Cambridge University Press, 1979.

——. "Scepticism and Toleration in the Seventeenth Century." In *Justifying Toleration*, ed. S. Mendus. Cambridge: Cambridge University Press: 21–36, 1988.

Van Bunge, Wiep. *From Stevin to Spinoza: An Essay on Philosophy in the Seventeenth-Century Dutch Republic*. Leiden: Brill, 2001.

Verbeek, Theo. *Spinoza's Theologico-Political Treatise: Exploring "the Will of God"*. Aldershot: Ashgate, 2003.

Waldron, Jeremy. "Locke: Toleration and the Rationality of Persecution." In *Justifying Toleration*, ed. S. Mendus. Cambridge: Cambridge University Press: 61–86, 1988.

160 BIBLIOGRAPHY

——. "The Wisdom of the Multitude: Some Reflections on Book 3, Chapter 11 of Aristotle's *Politics*." *Political Theory* 23: 563–84, 1995.

Wall, Steven. *Liberalism, Perfectionism, and Restraint*. Cambridge: Cambridge University Press, 1998.

——. "The Structure of Perfectionist Toleration." In *Perfectionism and Neutrality: Essays in Liberal Theory*, ed. S. Wall and G. Klosko. Lanham, MD: Rowman & Littlefield: 231–55, 2003.

Waller, Jason. *Persistence through Time in Spinoza*. Lanham, MD: Rowman & Littlefield, 2012.

West, David. "Spinoza on Positive Freedom." *Political Studies* 41: 284–96, 1993.

Williams, David Lay. "Spinoza and the General Will." *Journal of Politics* 72: 341–56, 2010.

Wright, Quincy. *A Study of War*, vol. 1. Chicago: University of Chicago Press, 1942.

Youpa, Andrew. "Spinozistic Self-Preservation." *Southern Journal of Philosophy* 41: 477–90, 2003.

Yovel, Yirmiahu. "Bible Interpretation as Philosophical Praxis: A Study of Spinoza and Kant." *Journal of the History of Philosophy* 11: 189–212, 1973.

INDEX

absolute miracle 58
Adam and Eve, Fall 75–6
American constitutional law
    122–3
animal behavior 23, 25, 26
anxiety 35, 36, 39
Aquinas, Thomas 7, 18, 60, 113
Aramaic 7, 87
arbitrary interference, freedom
    from 37
Aristotle 66, 80
atheism 49, 93, 99, 106
audience for Spinoza's works,
    intended 82–3
Austin, John 113, 114
authority: executive 16; and freedom
    32; justification of political 29, 31,
    43; religious, as subordinate to
    political power 46, 92, 109–19;
    sovereign *see* sovereign authority;
    of State 30
Averroes 81

Bible: biblical languages 7; Genesis
    68–9, 75; philosophical teachings of
    different biblical authors 85–6; as
    revolutionary text 6; scientific-
    historical method of interpretation
    (Spinoza) 82; supernaturalist
    readings 50; truth, questions of 80;
    and Universal Religion 94; *see also*
    God; Scripture(s); traditional
    biblical religion
biblical religion, traditional *see*
    traditional biblical religion
bondage xii; and civil society 39, 43,
    44; and freedom 29, 34; to the
    passions 134, 140;social contract
    theory 31; and state of nature 35, 36,
    37, 44; *see also* slavery

Catholic Church: in Christendom
    Model 3–4; importance in everyday
    life (Europe) 4; Scripture,
    interpretation 77, 78

162 INDEX

causal determinism (of Spinoza) 21
centralized states 2, 5–9,133
ceremonies, religious 75
Chaplinsky v. New Hampshire
(1942) 123
Charles of Habsburg 8
Christendom Model 2–5, 148;
challenges to 2–3, 5–6, 9, 10, 133;
collapse 151; Spinoza's arguments
as direct threat to 46; State
independent from but cooperating
with Church to form single organic
and unified political society 2, 4, 6,
11, 47; and toleration 108, 109, 122;
traditional biblical religion in 47–8;
transition to Liberal Republican
Model 10–11; Universal Religion 91
Church: Catholic 3–4, 77; independent
from but cooperating with State to
form single organic and unified
political society (Christendom
Model) 2, 4, 6, 11, 47; power in
pre-modern period 5; requirement
to perform vital functions for
secular rulers 4–5; undercutting
status of as result of Spinoza's
critique of religion 92; *see also*
Christendom Model; Protestant
Christianity
civic virtue, Universal Religion of
97–105
civil association, in state of nature 30
civil society 41, 122; and bondage 39,
43, 44; forming 42–4; and freedom
3, 29, 31, 42; need for 37–42
claim rights 16, 17; liberty rights
compared 15
conscience, freedom of 14, 122
Cooperation without Agreement,
Problem of 3, 10, 150

decentralization of power 10
De Cive (Hobbes) 19
Definition Argument 110, 115
deism 99

democratic theory 133–52; definition of
democracy 135–40; democracy vs.
aristocracy 138–9; direct democracy
139; diversity 134, 135, 148, 149–50,
151, 152, 164, 165; equality 140–1;
freedom 144–8; Liberal
Republicanism 3, 148–51; obedience
145, 146, 150, 151, 152; rationality
141–4, 143, 145; representative
republic 139; *see also* Liberal
Republicanism
Descartes, René 7, 64, 73
descriptive laws 17, 21
descriptive political theory 14
De Witt, Johan 9, 10
Dialogues Concerning Natural Religion
(Hume) 67
diversity 109; democratic theory 134,
135, 148, 149–50, 151, 152, 164, 165;
religious 9, 10, 93, 96, 97, 105, 109,
129, 130, 133, 147
divine law 26; Spinoza's foundational
claims 47, 71–7
Divine Natural Right Argument 17,
21–2, 27
dogmas: democratic theory 134, 149;
divine uniqueness 99–100; pious
97; practical 102; public or private
97; toleration 108, 119, 120, 122, 125,
126, 128; in Universal Religion 93,
97–106
Dutch Republic, seventeenth century 9,
10, 134

early modern period 2, 11; composite
states 8–9; crisis 5–9; foundational
claims 48
emotions 34, 103; *see also* passions
Enlightenment 83
*Enquiry Concerning Human
Understanding, An* (Hume) 58
Epistemic Thesis, defense 59, 63–8
equality, democratic 140–1
Ethics (Spinoza) 15; democratic theory
143, 147; effect of publication of *TTP*

INDEX 163

46; freedom and bondage 32–3; and miracles 60; naturalism 25; radical metaphysics in 50; reason, laws of 38, 40; state of nature 35, 36; toleration 126–7, 131; traditional biblical religion, critique 46, 50, 59, 60, 62, 63, 72, 73, 74; Universal Religion 100, 101, 103, 104

Evaluation Thesis 26

existence, universal struggle for (Spinoza) 15, 16, 17, 19, 21–2, 27

faith 6, 9, 50, 51, 77, 109, 123, 124, 129; confessional 130; defined by Spinoza 96; public 92, 94–102, 104–6

fear 30, 31, 35, 36, 39, 41

Federalist (Madison and Jay) 39, 143

Force of Law Argument 110, 112

foundational claims, Spinoza's alternative conception of society: divine law 47, 71–7; miracles 47, 57–70; prophecy (or revelation) 47, 48–57; Scripture, interpretation 47, 77–89

freedom: and absence of law 37; and authority 32; and bondage 32–5; and civil society 3, 29, 31, 42; of conscience 14, 122; democratic theory 144–8; as matter of degree 35; negative (freedom from interference) 31, 37; from passions 39, 40; positive (participatory) 3; and rationality 31, 33, 41; rejection by Spinoza of Hobbes' conception of 29, 31; republican 37; of speech 108, 122–3, 126; Spinoza on 29, 31, 32, 37; in state of nature 28, 29, 30, 31, 37; of thought and expression 1–2

freethinkers 46, 82, 93

free will 25, 32

Galileo 78

General Will 38, 143

Genesis 68–9, 75

God 16, 33, 50; belief in 98–9; confused idea of, alleged 64, 65; decrees 61; existence of, proof issues 58, 64, 65–6, 67; identity of will and intellect 60–1; inadequate understanding of, alleged 59, 64, 74; knowledge and love of 72, 73, 100, 106; and natural law/Natural Rights Thesis 18, 19, 22–3; omnipresent 100–1; and prophecy 50, 51, 52; Word of God, Scriptures as 47, 77, 78, 81; worship of 84, 102–3, 104, 105, 119; *see also* divine law; Divine Natural Right Argument; religion; traditional biblical religion; Universal Religion

Golden Rule 149

Gregory VII (Hildebrand), Pope 5

Grotius, Hugo 18, 19

Guide of the Perplexed (Maimonides) 72

Hart, H. L. A. 114

heaven and hell 103

Hebrew Bible 48–56, 68, 69; *see also* Judaism; traditional biblical religion

Hebrew language 7, 86, 87

Henry VI (Holy Roman Emperor) 5

heterogeneous societies 2, 9, 11–12

Hobbes, Thomas 14, 18, 45, 117–18, 136; freedom 31; *Leviathan* 16, 17, 110, 118; religion 45, 46; state of nature 28, 30, 35, 110

Hobbes, Thomas (writings): *De Cive* 19; *Leviathan* 16, 17

homogeneous societies 2, 4

Hooker, Richard 18

House of Orange 9, 135

human beings, and Natural Rights Thesis 23

human laws 72, 112

Hume, David 67; Humean miracle 58

hypothetical imperatives, prudential 19

164 INDEX

imagination 54; compared to intellect 53, 75
innovation: philosophical 2, 7; religious 2, 5–9
Inquisition 95–6
institutional religion 50, 57, 88, 89
institutions: political 4, 47, 70; religious 3, 94, 96, 97, 118, 119
intellect, compared to imagination 53, 75
interference, freedom from 31, 37
intolerance 109, 122, 125, 126, 127, 131, 150
Israel, Jonathan 6, 7, 46

Jellis, Jarig 29
Jesus Christ 56, 69, 85
joy 34
Judaism: and divine law 74; expulsion of Spinoza from Jewish community in Amsterdam for heresy (1656) 49; Jewish background of Spinoza 2; referral to God in 49, 50
justice 3; absence of 36; and charity 124–5

Kantian imperatives 19
knowledge, Cartesian assumptions 64

law(s): absence of 37; civil 113; defined 71; descriptive 17, 21; divine law 26, 47, 71–7; enforcement 30, 41; Force of Law Argument 110, 112; human 72, 112; irrational and immoral 113; moral 18, 19; positive (human-made) 14, 17, 18, 20, 21; punishment, threat of 30, 41; purpose of 71–2; of reason 38, 39, 40, 44; restrictive 126, 127–8; rule of law 136, 138, 139; rules for living 71–2; unreasonable 42; *see also* natural laws; natural law theory; nature, laws of; non-theistic natural law theory; theistic natural law theory

legal conformity, and piety 116
Legal Positivism 113, 114
legitimacy, political 4, 5, 30, 43, 92, 151, 152; Problem of Political Legitimacy 3, 10, 150
Leibniz, Gottfried Wilhelm 7
Letter Concerning Toleration (Locke) 107, 129
Letter to the Hebrews 87
Leviathan (Hobbes) 16, 17, 110, 118
Liberal Republicanism 3, 133, 148–51, 149; transition from Christendom Model 10–11; *see also* democratic theory
liberty rights: claim rights compared 15–16; in Natural Rights Thesis 17, 21–2, 27
Locke, John 7, 14, 29, 37, 117, 118; *Letter Concerning Toleration* 107, 129; religious toleration 107, 128–33; *Second Treatise on Government* 16, 37; state of nature 28, 30, 36
Luther, Martin 5, 6, 77, 78

Machiavelli, Niccolò 37, 149
Madison, James 38–9, 143–4
Maimonides, Moses 51, 53–4, 60, 72
majority, tyranny of 137
Matthew, Gospel of 87
Meditations (Descartes) 73
Metaphysical Thesis, defense 59, 59–63
metaphysics 48, 50, 55, 100, 104, 134
Meyer, Lodewijk 78, 80–1
"might makes right," claim of 13, 14, 17, 27
Mill, John Stuart 137
miracles: absolute 58; and critique of traditional biblical religion by Spinoza 47, 57–70; defense of Epistemic Thesis 59, 63–8; defense of Metaphysical Thesis 59, 59–63; defense of Scriptural Thesis 59, 68–70; existing religious hierarchy, critique intended to undermine 70; God, understanding of 58–9;

INDEX 165

Humean 58; misguided belief in the possibility of 63; relative 57, 58
Moderate Enlightenment 7
monarchy 8, 147; monarchists/anti-monarchists 10
Montesquieu, Charles-Louis de Secondat 37, 117, 118
moral censure 25
moralistic and amoralistic natural law theory 19–20, 23–4, 27
moral law 18, 19
Moses/Mosaic prophecy 53, 56, 67, 85, 114

Nadler, Steven 45–6
naturalism 14, 26, 27, 31, 134; and Natural Rights Thesis 23–4; traditional biblical religion, critique 50, 60; see also metaphysics
natural laws 14, 20; Hobbesian 18–19; moral 18, 19; prescriptive 17–18
natural law theory: moralistic 19–20, 23–4, 27; non-theistic 18–20, 21; rejection in Natural Rights Thesis 14; theistic 18, 20; violation of natural law 18
Natural Rights Thesis 13, 14; ability to survive in universal struggle for existence coextensive with liberty right to do anything believed to be useful in that struggle 17, 21–2, 27; applicable to animals and human beings 23; and naturalism 14, 23–4; power and natural right 15–17
nature, laws of 14, 17, 20, 23, 112; and divine law 72, 75; Metaphysical Thesis, defense 61–2; violation of 57, 65; see also divine law
negative freedom 31
Newton, Isaac 7
Nietzsche, Friedrich 15
Ninety-Five Theses (Luther) 5
Noah (biblical figure) 68–9
Non-Contradiction, Principle of 65

non-theistic natural law theory 18–20, 21; moralistic and amoralistic 19–20, 23–4, 27; see also natural law theory; theistic natural law theory
normative political theory 14

obedience 3, 31, 73; democratic theory 145, 146, 150, 151, 152; and need for civil society 41, 42, 44; toleration 114, 116; Universal Religion 94, 95, 96, 98, 100, 102
Of the Laws of Ecclesiastical Polity (Hooker) 18
Orangists 9, 134–5
ownership, and claim rights 16

Parmenides 61
participatory (positive) freedom 3
passions 31, 33, 146; arbitrary and random 38, 142–3; bondage to 43, 134, 140; checking 126–7; external causes 34; freedom from 39, 40, 43
paternalism 146
Peace of Westphalia (1648) 8, 9, 11, 109
philosophy: natural, as science 78; philosophical innovation, rise in 2, 7; prophets compared to philosophers 54
Philosophy as the Interpreter of Holy Scripture (Meyer) 80–1
piety 49, 50, 82, 87, 88, 150; toleration 115, 116, 121, 131; Universal Religion 95, 96
Pinker, Steven 8
Plato 13, 51, 53
pleasure 34
pluralism, religious and scientific 2, 3, 9, 11
Political Legitimacy Problem 3, 10, 150
political power: concentration of 2; religious authority subordinate to 46, 92, 109–19; see also power

166 INDEX

Political Treatise (*PT*), Spinoza 22, 39, 137, 141; state of nature and social contract theory 33, 35

politics: Bible, political influence 6; Church involvement with (prior to Reformation) 6; justification of political authority 29, 31, 43; natural right, definition 15; political centralization and religious innovation 2, 5–9, 133; political dissolution 118; political power *see* political power; seventeenth-century debates 1–2; Theological-Political Problem 3, 9–11; weakly normative political theory (Spinoza) 14, 24–6; *see also* religion

positive (human-made) laws 14, 17, 18, 20, 21

positive (participatory) freedom 3

power: "checks and balances" system 117; concentration of 11; decentralization of 10; definition by Spinoza as universal ability to survive in struggle for existence 15, 16, 17, 19, 21–2, 27; and natural right 14, 15–17, 31; political *see* political power; sovereign, natural limits 119–25

pre-modern period, power of Church in 5

prescriptive natural laws 17–18

Prescriptive Thesis 25, 26

Principle of Sufficient Reason 65

prophecy 48–57; and critique of traditional biblical religion by Spinoza 47; definitions 51; deflationary account 50, 53; epistemological uniqueness of prophets, removal 52; false prophets 67; in Hebrew Bible 48–56; and human mind 52, 53; and Jesus Christ 56, 69, 85; metaphysics 48, 50, 55; moral certainty 55; moral teachers, prophets as 56, 57; Moses/Mosaic prophecy 53, 56, 67, 85, 114; philosophers and prophets 54; radical conclusions 48, 50, 51; rhetoric 49, 57; role of prophet 51, 56, 57; and toleration 111–12

Protestant Christianity 49; Reformation 2, 5–6, 7, 77

psychology 31, 36, 37, 126; democratic theory 142, 144, 146

public faith 92, 94–102, 104–6; dogmas 93, 98–106; *see also* dogmas; faith

rationality: democratic theory 141–4, 143, 145; and freedom 31, 33, 41

reason: and difference 40; and disagreement 39–40; laws of 38, 39, 40, 44; and prophecy 52; rule of 31; unreasonable laws, obedience to 42

relative miracle 57, 58

religion: external and internal 92; institutional 50, 57, 88, 89; internal religious beliefs, separating from external religious practices 93–7; religious authority as subordinate to political power 46, 92, 109–19; seventeenth-century debates 1–2; toleration 107–32; traditional biblical, critique *see* traditional biblical religion; Universal *see* Universal Religion; *see also* Christendom Model; God; religious innovation; religious sectarianism; religious traditionalists; Wars of Religion

religious diversity 9, 10; democratic theory 133, 147; toleration 109, 129, 130; Universal Religion 93, 96, 97, 105

religious innovation 2, 5–9

religious institutions 3, 94, 96, 97, 118, 119; *see also* institutional religion

religious sectarianism 6, 7, 122

religious traditionalists 10

religious wars 2, 6, 109

Republic (Plato) 13

INDEX 167

restrictive laws 126, 127–8
revelation *see* prophecy, critique of traditional biblical religion by Spinoza
rights 138; claim 15, 16,17; common 16,40; individual 138; *see also* liberty rights; Natural Rights Thesis
rituals, religious 75
Roman Empire *see* Western Roman Empire
Rousseau, Jean-Jacques 122, 149; civil society 37, 43; General Will 143; state of nature and social contract theory 28, 29, 35, 36
rule of law 136, 138, 139

sadness 34, 35
salvation 56, 78, 129, 130; Universal Religion 95, 103, 104, 105
Schenck v. United States (1919) 123
Scriptural Thesis, defense 59, 68–70
Scripture(s) 6–7, 75; Epistemic Thesis, defense 67, 68; as historical narrative 80, 83–4; interpretation 7, 47, 77–89; and Universal Religion 94; as Word of God 47, 77, 78, 81; *see also* Bible; religion; traditional biblical religion; Universal Religion
Second Treatise on Government (Locke) 16, 37
sectarianism, religious 6, 7, 122
self-destruction, impossibility of 15
self-preservation and power 15, 16, 17, 19, 21–2
seventeenth-century: debates, religious and political 1–2; Dutch Republic 9
Short Treatise on God, Man, and His Well-Being (Spinoza) 32
signs 55, 57–9
skepticism 60, 73, 78, 127, 129, 130
slavery 29, 43; *see also* bondage
social collapse 131, 134
Social Contract (Rousseau) 122
social contract theory 44; classical 29–32, 43, 44; as justification for State

authority 30; language of classical social contract theorists 43; Spinoza on 31–2, 43, 44; and state of nature 28–9; weakly normative political theory (Spinoza) 29, 43; *see also* state of nature
sovereign authority 117, 118, 127, 130, 134, 137; absolute 119; Sovereign Authority Argument 110, 116; *see also* authority; sovereign power
sovereign power 43, 114, 131; natural limits 119–25; *see also* sovereign authority
speech, freedom of 108, 122–3, 126
Spinoza, Benedict (Baruch) (philosophy) 2, 3; alternative conception of political society 47; criticism of existing power structures 14; freedom 29, 31, 32, 36, 37; positive account of proper role of religion in State 46, 70; power, definition 15, 16, 17; reason, laws of 38; rejection of traditional religion 7, 46; religious toleration 128–33; social contract theory 31–2, 43; state of nature 35–6; and Theological-Political Problem 10; weakly normative political theory *see* weakly normative political theory (Spinoza)
Spinoza, Benedict (Baruch) (writings): *Ethics see Ethics* (Spinoza); *Political Treatise (PT)* 22, 33, 35, 39, 137, 141; *Short Treatise on God, Man, and His Well-Being* 32; *Theological-Political Treatise (TTP) see Theological-Political Treatise (TTP)* (Spinoza); *Treatise on the Emendation of the Intellect* 32, 48
stadholder (royal general) 9
State 5, 30, 45, 149; independent from but cooperating with Church to form single organic and unified political society (Christendom Model) 2, 4, 6, 11, 47; positive

168 INDEX

account of proper role of religion in 46, 70; *see also* Christendom Model

state of nature 35–7, 44, 140; anxiety and fear, living in 30, 31, 35, 36; and bondage 35, 36, 37, 44; and civil society 41; and freedom 28, 29, 30, 31, 37; Hobbes on 28, 30, 35; insecurity and violence in 30, 31, 35; lack of ownership or private property in 36; Locke on 28, 30, 36; pre-political 30; and slavery 29; and social contract theory 28–9; Spinoza on 29, 35–7; State of Nature Argument 110–11; *see also* social contract theory

Statists 9, 10

striving, and power 15

suicide 15

Summa Theologiae (Aquinas) 18, 113

summum bonum (highest human good) 72, 73, 76, 95, 100, 148

supernatural knowledge *see* prophecy (or revelation), critique of traditional biblical religion

superstition 31

survival instinct, and power 15, 16, 17, 21–2

theistic natural law theory 18, 20; *see also* non-theistic natural law theory

Theological-Political Problem 3, 9–11; and Cooperation without Agreement, Problem of 3, 10, 150; and Political Legitimacy Problem 3, 10, 150

Theological-Political Treatise (TTP), Spinoza 10, 26, 39, 107; anonymous publication 45, 46; attacks on 46, 83; banning of 45; biblical hermeneutics 50; democratic theory 139, 142; intended audience 82–3; naturalism and Natural Rights Thesis 20–1, 22; power and natural right 13, 14, 15; Preface 82; state of nature and social contract theory 31,

35; subtitle 107; toleration 109–15, 119–22, 124, 126; traditional biblical religion, critique 45–7, 49–76, 78, 79, 81–4, 86–9; Universal Religion 96, 98

Thirty Years War (1618–45) 8

tolerance xi, 3, 94, 149, 150, 152; and toleration 102, 103, 131

toleration 3, 9; Christendom Model 108, 109, 122; Definition Argument 110, 115; definitions 108; Divine Natural Right Argument 17, 21–2, 27; dogmas 108, 119, 120, 122, 125, 126, 128; Force of Law Argument 110, 112; Locke on 107, 128–33; as necessary for a virtuous citizenry 125–8; religious authority as subordinate to political power 109–19; Sovereign Authority Argument 110, 116; sovereign power, natural limits 119–25; Spinoza's views compared with Locke 128–33; State of Nature Argument 110–11

totalitarianism 111

traditional biblical religion: challenging of foundations of biblical religion by Spinoza 7, 46, 48; in Christendom Model 47–8; critique by Spinoza 26, 45–90, 92, 93, 134; deemed unnecessary for a good life 75; Hobbes on 45, 46; and Moderate Enlightenment 7; universalizing tendency of Spinoza in his critique 48; and Universal Religion 105–6; *see also* Bible; foundational claims, Spinoza's alternative conception of society; God; religion; Scripture(s); Universal Religion

translation of Bible 6

Treatise on the Emendation of the Intellect (Spinoza) 32, 48

TTP see Theological-Political Treatise (TTP), Spinoza

tyranny of the majority 137

INDEX 169

Universal Religion 84, 91–106, 108, 114, 150; Christendom Model 91; of civic virtue 97–105; dogmas in 93, 97–105; internal religious beliefs, separating from external religious practices 93–7; public faith 92, 94–102, 104–6; religious diversity 93, 96, 97, 105; salvation 95, 103, 104, 105; *see also* Bible; faith; God; religion; Scripture(s); traditional biblical religion

virtues: civic 97–105; liberal republican 3

Wars of Religion 2, 6, 109
weakly normative political theory (Spinoza) 14, 24–6, 105, 138; Evaluation Thesis 26; Prescriptive Thesis 25, 26; and social contract theory 29, 43
Western Roman Empire: collapse (fifth century) 2, 3, 5
Westphalia, Peace of (1648) 8, 9, 11, 109
William II (Prince of Orange) 9
Word of God, Scriptures as 47, 77, 78, 81
worship 84, 102–3, 104, 105, 119
Wright, Quincy 8

eBooks
from Taylor & Francis
Helping you to choose the right eBooks for your Library

Add to your library's digital collection today with Taylor & Francis eBooks. We have over 50,000 eBooks in the Humanities, Social Sciences, Behavioural Sciences, Built Environment and Law, from leading imprints, including Routledge, Focal Press and Psychology Press.

Free Trials Available

We offer free trials to qualifying academic, corporate and government customers.

Choose from a range of subject packages or create your own!

Benefits for you
- Free MARC records
- COUNTER-compliant usage statistics
- Flexible purchase and pricing options
- 70% approx of our eBooks are now DRM-free.

Benefits for your user
- Off-site, anytime access via Athens or referring URL
- Print or copy pages or chapters
- Full content search
- Bookmark, highlight and annotate text
- Access to thousands of pages of quality research at the click of a button.

eCollections

Choose from 20 different subject eCollections, including:

- Asian Studies
- Economics
- Health Studies
- Law
- Middle East Studies

eFocus

We have 16 cutting-edge interdisciplinary collections, including:

- Development Studies
- The Environment
- Islam
- Korea
- Urban Studies

For more information, pricing enquiries or to order a free trial, please contact your local sales team:

UK/Rest of World: **online.sales@tandf.co.uk**
USA/Canada/Latin America: **e-reference@taylorandfrancis.com**
East/Southeast Asia: **martin.jack@tandf.com.sg**
India: **journalsales@tandfindia.com**

www.tandfebooks.com